Practical Wisdom

Practical Wisdom

The Seeker's Guide to a Meaningful Life

FRANK MALLINDER

Practical Wisdom
The Seeker's Guide to a Meaningful Life

iUniverse books may be ordered through booksellers or by contacting:

iUniverse
1663 Liberty Drive
Bloomington, IN 47403
www.iuniverse.com
1-800-Authors (1-800-288-4677)

Because of the dynamic nature of the Internet, any web addresses or links contained in this book may have changed since publication and may no longer be valid. The views expressed in this work are solely those of the author and do not necessarily reflect the views of the publisher, and the publisher hereby disclaims any responsibility for them.

Any people depicted in stock imagery provided by Thinkstock are models, and such images are being used for illustrative purposes only.
Certain stock imagery © Thinkstock.

ISBN: 978-1-4620-4051-3 (sc)
ISBN: 978-1-4620-4053-7 (hc)
ISBN: 978-1-4620-4052-0 (e)

Library of Congress Control Number: 2011913680

Print information available on the last page.

iUniverse rev. date: 06/01/2015

To my wonderful kids, Troy Mallidner, Jari Peters, Jason Mallinder, and Brian Mallinder

Life is a never-ending series of temporary events.

—Frank Mallinder

Acknowledgments

I would like to thank all of the clients I've worked with over the years for the wonderful insights I have gained from them and for allowing me to be myself and do what I love to do, which is coach. Jan Janke and Mickie Zada have played a vital role in my writing process. Without them, I would still be contemplating whether or not I would complete this book. Thank you!

All of the clients' names that appear in this book have been changed to protect their privacy. Some of the examples I use are compilations of several different client experiences.

CONTENTS

Introduction

Do You Need Another Self-Insight Book?

As I picked up the phone to answer the call, my palms were a little moist—I was nervous. It was my normal response to beginning work with a new coaching client named Joan. The phone had rung exactly at ten in the morning, which was the time we had agreed upon for our first coaching call. I like clients who are prompt.

When I said hello to Joan, I began to relax and build a connection with her. After reviewing a few key points about the coaching process, I asked Joan to talk for a few minutes about what she wanted to gain from the coaching. She said, "I am forty-nine years old, my kids are grown and gone from home, my job is not fulfilling, and quite frankly, my marriage has some problems. I have read lots of books, listened to many audio programs, and gone to numerous seminars. I am not new to the concept of self-insight. I feel stuck. What I need is help with my time-management skills so that I spend less time in the family business and more time doing what I love to do, which is to conduct motivational seminars. I know I have more to offer the world. I have an ache in my soul. I have talents that haven't been fully engaged. I want the next part of my life to be different from the last part. I just know I have something more to contribute to the world. *I want* to change my life!"

Joan's words represent the essence of what I hear from virtually all of my clients. Joan is the reason why I do what I do, which is coach and write. She knows she has untapped potential, and she is ready to experience what life is like when she taps into her real self. In short, she is ready to live a life that matches her talents and capabilities. She knows that something is not working in her life. Something is holding her back, and she is ready to deal with it. Joan is what I call a seeker. A seeker is someone who is and always will be learning and ready to take action on what she has learned. On the other end of the spectrum are the people I call the dreamers. Dreamers learn all through their lives but never do anything with their knowledge. They just dream and perhaps even complain about what is not happening in their lives. Having untapped potential is a positive thing—it's not the same as saying that someone has an awful life or is completely down on his or her luck. Some of my clients are down on their luck and some are very well off. What they have in common is an ache inside that they want to stop. They want more pure joy in their lives.

This book is for anyone who wants to stop the ache and live a purposeful, high-energy life that fully engages their talents. In this book I share with you practical bits of wisdom that will help you make the "Big Change" you may have been reluctant to make for most of your life. The "Big Change" is the secret you have kept to yourself about what you really want to do with your life but have been fearful of tackling.

The Big Change Joan really wanted to make was to embrace her desire to leave the family business and start a company that focused on inspiring women to live a fuller life. She had a talent for listening to others and speaking in ways that other women could hear. However, Joan had been brought up to always put the needs of the family first. Her husband was not good at managing the details of their family business, so he needed Joan to do it as well as take care of business emergencies. He could hire someone else, but he didn't feel he could trust anyone but Joan. He needed her. Joan felt trapped in the business and couldn't see a way to get out without violating her responsibility to her family. She could not find the courage to tell her husband what she really wanted to do. All of her life Joan had secretly wanted to be independent and have a career of her own focused on teaching and motivating others. When I met Joan the ache inside her was huge, and she hid it well.

To those outside of the family business, it seemed as if Joan had it all—a nice home, great children, a successful husband and business, and an active role in the community. This was all true, but she was missing the most important element of a meaningful life—doing something that is truly meaningful and makes use of all of one's talents.

This book is about facing the fear of making the Big Change and figuring out how your talents can be used and challenged every day. The most important thing this book will teach you is how to eliminate the fear that stands between you and a truly fulfilled life. Once the fear is removed, you will learn how to sustain the real you for the rest of your life. Things don't create a meaningful life; being who you really are at the soul level creates a meaningful life.

If you are like me, right about now you are having the following silent discussion with yourself: *I already have two and half large bookcases full of self-insight books; do I really need another one? This one* does *look very interesting—I wonder if it has the answer for why I have been struggling to create exactly what I want in my life? It may just be the one for which I have been searching. I hope it is.*

Going through this self-imposed inquisition about book buying can be very trying. Let me offer you several thoughts on why you should read this one:

- You *do* need another book on self-insight. Not because the others didn't work, but because as a seeker, you will always need another book. Seekers always need to learn, grow, and create. If you stop reading, your growth and creativity will come to a halt. Your soul needs to be nourished on a daily basis. *Practical Wisdom* is your guide to creating joy and abundance in your life by aligning all the parts of you so that there is no way you will die with the music still inside.

- Our souls are like the tires on a bicycle. Regular maintenance is required. What happens to the ride on the bike if you don't maintain the correct pressure in the tires? The tires slowly lose air, and it gets harder to pedal the bike. Our lives are the same way. Life gets much harder when we don't nourish our souls, keep our faith alive, and keep our souls pumped up. Reading self-insight/spiritual books is one of the ways in which you can nurture your soul.

- *Practical Wisdom* is intended to show you that your tires have probably never been inflated to the correct pressure. I will show you how to determine what the correct pressure is for you and how to maintain it so you will have a much smoother ride for the rest of your life. You will learn to create life patterns that are high energy, soul-enriching, and in alignment with your talents. Any lack of clarity about your mission in life will be eliminated.

A while ago this quote, attributed to professional motorcycle racer Bill McKenna, was e-mailed to me by three different people in a less than a week. I believe it expresses what I want from life and what my clients desire. See if it matches what you want.

"Life is not a journey to the grave with the intention of arriving safely in a pretty and well preserved body, but rather to skid in broadside, thoroughly used up, totally worn out, and loudly proclaiming 'Wow! What a ride!'"

I have coached many seekers who know that they have not yet fully engaged their talents. They know there is more for them to do, and they are determined to experience the exhilaration of living full out.

I coached a very successful dentist who specialized in creating beautiful smiles, and by dentistry standards she was at the top of her career. Yet there was more she wanted to do. She wanted to build a magnificent retreat center and be a spiritual teacher and coach. Her soul has been aching to do this, and she is now in the process of creating it.

A very talented sales consultant who is excellent at teaching people what to say when they are selling is very dissatisfied with his life. He wants to more fully engage his spirit. He has a similar goal to the dentist. He now has plans to build a wonderful place for spiritual authors to come for marketing assistance to get their messages out to the world. It will also be a place where authors can conduct seminars on their material.

A self-employed business owner participated in my teleclasses because she knew that she was capable of being a powerful leader, but she needed to find the courage to step up to her full leadership potential. She is now doing that and having a powerful impact on her organization.

I could fill a book with stories like these about what other clients have achieved. The practical wisdom I share in these pages played a pivotal role in the successes I have described. I believe in the magnificent potential of mankind. If you desire to do it, I know that it is possible to engage your life at a higher level. I am not suggesting that everyone can save the world. However, I am suggesting that there is more we can put into and take from life. I know that you can lead a meaningful life.

As you read through *Practical Wisdom,* I encourage you to continually ask yourself, *What does this sentence mean to my life?* This will help you identify the practical wisdom that is meaningful to you.

Here's the bottom line: if you are ready to fully engage your talents and live a life that I like to call "peacefully supercharged," then dive into this book and begin applying what you learn. This book is about "tuning your soul" so that the energy of the universe flows naturally through you and produces the Energy of Success. Yes, it is hard work. Television has taught us that every problem can be solved in thirty to sixty minutes. Tuning your soul to create the Energy of Success takes more than thirty minutes. Seekers are aware that tuning must be done frequently, and the amount of time it will take depends on how far out of alignment your life has become from your mission in life.

To maximize your investment in the time spent reading this book, there are two things you will need: a pencil and sticky notes. The pencil is to mark your practical wisdom in this book. The sticky notes are for creating reminders that you can put in lots of places as triggers to help you do what you committed to doing for a meaningful life.

Buckle up; your Big Change process is about to begin.

Chapter 1

Caution: You Are about to Enter the Big Change Zone

Pete finished running his first marathon a few days before our twelfth coaching session. He was an eager student and a fast learner whom I coached for many months. What a different person he was in the twelfth session from the first time we talked! During his first coaching session, he said to me, "My goal for the coaching process is to be disciplined enough to pay off all of my debts, including my mortgage. I want to be able to enjoy a peaceful retirement with my wife." There was very little energy/excitement in his voice as he talked about his life and his goals. When I inquired about his debts and mortgage, I discovered that they weren't really a large percentage of his income, and the goal wasn't much of a stretch. The real issue was that Pete wasn't enjoying his life. He was bored and feeling unfulfilled even though he had a good job, a loving wife, and two wonderful toys: a motorcycle and sailboat. Like many of my over-forty clients, he was trying to fill the infamous hole in the soul, and he thought that getting coaching on a goal he perceived to be important would energize his life. The actual problem was that his real identity had gotten lost over the years, and he was not living a meaningful life. His real talents were not being used. Pete is a creative person who was drowning in a routine, rule-bound job as an internal auditor. He loves traveling, taking photos, exercising outdoors, and giving back to his community, and he had a strong desire to visit Ireland, which is the homeland of his father.

None of these things were currently present in his life. In essence, the things that would create a meaningful life for him were missing.

Leading a meaningful life is much harder work than most self-insight gurus would lead you to believe. In my experience, most people aren't concerned about leading a meaningful life until they are forty-plus years old. Prior to that they believe that the activities that fill their planners are what create meaning. Their motto is *"A busy life is a meaningful life."* Some people eventually realize that all of the things that consume their days do nothing to eliminate the emptiness and ache they feel for not fully being who they were sent here to be.

There is no digital device, no matter how frequently you use it or intently you monitor it that will soothe an aching soul.

My clients are generally surprised when they realize what it takes to create a life that is peacefully supercharged. You will know that you are peacefully supercharged when you feel the energy that comes from knowing and living your mission. You have the peace from clearly knowing who you are, and your energy is fueled by the excitement of fulfilling your mission. To attain a peacefully supercharged life, you must be ready to make a Big Change. By Big Change, I mean a change that will transform your life. It is the change that leads to the authentic you. The Big Change is what you do when you are ready to fully utilize all of your talents and live your life's mission.

Pete made the Big Change. During our twelfth coaching session, as I listened to him bubble over about the wonderful experience he had in the marathon, I felt privileged to be his coach. Pete had mastered all of things I believe are necessary to live out his potential in a meaningful way. He ran that marathon for two reasons. One was that he enjoys running and wanted to test his running skills in a marathon. The second and perhaps more significant reason was that he wanted to add meaning to his life by raising money for the Leukemia and Lymphoma Society. He raised over $2,000.

Pete has broken out of his self-imposed subconscious fear-based restraints and is living the life of a creative and adventurous individual. He was able to transition from a life that was an incomplete match to his potential to one that is becoming a perfect match for his talents. He is finding meaning in all areas of his life where before there was little or no meaning. Instead of the relatively small and easy goal of paying off debt, Pete went for the Big Change and is now experiencing his talents and living a meaningful life. He's also making plans to visit Ireland.

Caution: You Are about to Enter the "Big Change" Zone

There are four major character traits required to make the Big Change. I identified these traits earlier when I considered what led my clients to success in making their Big Change. It just so happens that all of the traits begin with the letter C.

The four Cs of Big Change are as follows:

- Courage
- Clarity
- Commitment
- Compassion

Without the four Cs of Big Change,

- creating a peacefully supercharged, meaningful, and talent-driven life will not be obtainable or sustainable;
- implementing the practical wisdom I detail in this book (or implementing anything you read on self-insight for that matter) will be very difficult.

Let's look at each one of the four Cs.

Courage

Courage is perhaps the most important one of the four Cs. I define courage as the willingness to do things that the average person won't. Creating a joy-filled life requires that you look at parts of your life that you couldn't or wouldn't look at before. As you examine each part of your life, you must be ready to be honest with yourself about whether it is working or not. Courage also requires actions that may be uncomfortable and disruptive to life as you know it. *To stop the cycle of doing the same things over and over again and expecting a different result, you must have the courage to do things differently.*

In order to run the marathon, Pete had to have the courage to do things differently than before. He had to create a training schedule that was much more rigorous than he had ever experienced. He had to have the courage to continue training even when it would have been easier to sit at home after a long day at work. Because he was training, his wife was upset that he wasn't always at home as he once was. He had to have the courage to face her displeasure with his workout schedule. Let me add that Pete wasn't neglecting his wife; he just wasn't there all of the time. (By the way, his wife is now running with him and they plan to run a half marathon together.)

Susan was a forty-eight-year-old client who unexpectedly found herself pregnant. She had one other child who was a junior in high school, and he no longer required untold amounts of time and attention. Her career was really taking off, and she was enjoying it a great deal. Her husband had his own business that was doing well. Susan thought that she was at the point in her life when she would have the freedom to do what she wanted. The unplanned pregnancy literally blew up all of her plans. It seemed to put a major kink in all of the things that she had worked on during our coaching sessions. Susan had a great deal of faith in God, and this was a major test of that faith. It took courage for her to examine what she was feeling versus what she believed in. This was the darkest, most difficult time of her life. The outcome of her courage was a wonderful daughter who has added immensely to the lives of Susan and her family.

When courage is absent as you embark on a Big Change, you will find yourself continually questioning the wisdom of your decision to go for it. Insufficient courage and an average life of low meaning sounds like, "I am comfortable where I am. Why push myself? Nobody will notice if I don't finish this. It doesn't matter anyway."

Courage is not something that you wake up with one morning and declare that you possess it. Courage is something you develop over time. You must create a solid foundation for your life in order to possess courage. In this book, you will learn things that will add to your level of courage and preparedness to live a meaningful life. There is no doubt in my mind that it takes courage to make the Big Change. Understanding the four Cs is one thing that will help open your eyes.

Commitment

Commitment is defined as the state or an instance of being obligated or emotionally impelled. When you are in the Big Change Zone, being emotionally impelled is mandatory. Anything less and you end up frustrated just as you have so many times in the past. Making the Big Change requires that you significantly alter what you have stored in your subconscious mind. What most people refer to as commitment is the willingness to say yes to what you think someone else wants you to do. We seldom say yes to a commitment because we want it; we say yes to make other people happy and get them off our backs.

The positive-thinking gurus have trained us to say yes anytime they ask a question that is supposed to lead us to a brighter and more prosperous life, as if simply saying yes in a loud voice will result in a new behavior. For most people, they are no sooner out the door of the positive-thinking gurus' seminars when they can no longer generate the commitment to follow through on what they had loudly proclaimed they would do just thirty minutes earlier. How can you be emotionally impelled if part of your Big Change is to elevate your emotional energy to a level you have seldom experienced? Most people don't really know what commitment is or what it feels like. Being fully committed feels uncomfortable when you first experience it. Be prepared for the discomfort when you launch your Big Change.

During our coaching call, I asked Bill if he was really committed to doing what it would take to make his catering business take off. Was he ready to complete the business plan, set a budget and stick to it, make thousands of phone calls (he hated doing cold calls), and devote ten to twelve hours a day to it for the first year? So far Bill had a different excuse every coaching call for why he had delayed diving into doing the things he said he needed to do for the business. I asked the question about commitment on this coaching call because I wanted Bill to come face to face with his level of commitment. As soon as I asked about his level of commitment, Bill said in a very direct voice, "Yes!" However, I sensed less-than-full commitment, and I explained that it was okay to say no to the question. I asked him to tell me what was in his heart and not what he thought he should tell me. There was long pause. I took that as my cue to explain the difference between real commitment and fake commitment.

Within several weeks, Bill made a real commitment and charged full steam ahead with his business.

Commitment represents a state of internal energy that is imperturbable. When you are committed, you will do whatever it takes to maintain that level of energy. Most people mistake having an interest in something with making a commitment to it. The difference is immense. When you have an interest in something, it indicates that you would be happy to see your interest materialize. However, if it doesn't work out, that is okay, too. There is always a reason why you couldn't follow through.

If you asked me at any point in the past five years if I was committed to writing this book, I would have quickly responded yes. However, I wasn't. I had an interest in doing it, and I always had excuses as to why I wasn't working on it at the current time. Fear and procrastination were my constant subconscious companions on this book. It wasn't until late last year that I became committed to completing it. I realized that living my life's mission meant that I must complete and publish this book. When I realized that, the energy and creativity I put into it accelerated.

Here is a test you can use to determine if you are committed to a goal or an intention. Ask yourself, "What is the most important thing in my life that I intend to accomplish in the next ninety days? What am I going to accomplish toward the realization of my intention in the next seven days?" As you ask yourself these two questions, notice the energy you feel as you answer them. Did you feel a surge of power, or did you get a sinking feeling in the pit of your stomach and a reluctance to come up with answers? It you felt the latter, you are probably not committed. If you felt the former and you actually meet your seven-day goal, then you are committed to your intention. *There is no sin in not really being committed to a goal. The problem with fake commitment is that it generates guilt and anxiety as well as a diminished sense of self-worth when you don't follow through.* It is very difficult to fully commit to something when you lack **clarity** about who you are and what you really want from life.

Clarity

If you enter the Big Change Zone without clarity, you are doomed to wander around aimlessly while your frustration grows as you fail to reach your destination. Instituting changes that will help you create a more meaningful, joyful, and abundant life demands clarity on several different levels. The obvious one is that you must be very clear on what you want and why you want it. Secondly, it is important that you understand what your life's mission is and how the change will help fulfill it. The third aspect of clarity is that you must recognize the subconscious patterns that drive your behavior. You will need to understand which patterns are fear-based and what must change into in order to achieve your goal. Until you make the subconscious patterns changes, goal achievement will be nonexistent or short-lived.

When I started working with Jane, she was in a lot of emotional and spiritual pain. She had no mission statement, operated from fear-based patterns most of the time, and on every coaching call she wanted to focus on something different. First it was to find a job, then it was to be a leader in a service organization, then it was to be a writer, and the list goes on. All along the way we kept clarifying subconscious patterns and working on her mission statement. Slowly, clarity developed. The emotional and spiritual pain has been replaced with a feeling of joy, a clear direction for her career, and new power and joy in her writing.

I admire Jane a great deal because she had the courage to keep learning and looking at parts of her life that were not working. As fears were replaced with a strong sense of self, it became easier to make and keep commitments. Additionally, she no longer made commitments to things that don't fit with who she really is. What a release of energy that created. As her clarity evolved, her actions became bolder and more creative. The process has taken several years. When you enter the Big Change Zone, be prepared to spend more than thirty minutes getting to the answer. In three months you will have a solid start on your change. With commitment and the other three Cs, your Big Change will occur within six months to a year.

Compassion

The Dalai Lama is quoted as saying, "If you want others to be happy, practice compassion. If you want to be happy, practice compassion." If I may be so bold as to add to that statement, I suggest that if you want to be happy, you must not only be compassionate toward others, you must be compassionate toward yourself. Once you have learned to be truly compassionate toward yourself, then you can be more compassionate toward others.

Like Jane, whom I mentioned in the section on clarity, most of my clients have long-hidden, yet very powerful subconscious fear-based patterns that are the source of a never-ending barrage of negative self-talk. It is impossible to create a meaningful, mission-driven life if you don't love yourself. How can you create change if you are constantly criticizing what you are doing and thinking? How can you create joy and abundance if your constant companion is fear?

In order to be compassionate, you must be able to recognize what someone else is feeling and experiencing. I find that most people have a limited ability to recognize what it is they are feeling, let alone what someone else is feeling. By learning to fully understand what is happening inside of ourselves and celebrate our talents, we can become compassionate toward ourselves. Self-compassion leads to the release of a huge amount of energy that has been bottled up inside for too long. When you see yourself clearly and yet love yourself completely, then you will be overwhelmed at how compassionate you are toward others.

During a recent coaching session with Ruth, it became obvious that her relationship with her husband had dramatically improved. She was now able to see how much pain he was in as a result of his need to be constantly working and never resting. When we started our coaching, she was frequently upset about something he had failed to do for her because he was so busy at work. Over several months of coaching, Ruth was able to identify and change several of her own fear-based patterns. She learned to enjoy being herself and be compassionate with herself when things didn't go exactly as she had planned. One of the things she learned was that her fear caused her to be angry with herself and she would find ways to take that anger out on her husband. She realized that he had his own fears to deal with. Once this occurred, the tone of their interactions changed. Love was present again. I could actually hear a difference in her voice as she talked about her husband—all because she learned to have compassion for herself.

In my coaching, I teach my clients how to recognize life patterns that are propelled by fears that they learned much earlier in life. Life patterns that are rooted in fear separate us from fully experiencing our real and wonderful talents. Fear-based life patterns cause you to function at a level lower than your true capacity. They cause you to feel defective because you cannot execute the desires of your heart. In this book, you will see how creating a gap between stimulus and response will give you an opportunity to recognize when fears are taking hold and causing the real you to disappear. You can then make a conscious decision about your emotions and behavior, allowing compassion for yourself to emerge, and thus enhancing your ability to recognize what is happening to others. Really understanding others starts when you get you own fear out of the way and stop projecting them into your interactions with others.

Clearly, the four Cs of Big Change are critically important characteristics to have as you move through the Big Change Zone. Most people don't show up at coaching sessions possessing them. They develop them through the application of the practical wisdom I share with you in the pages to come. If you know about them as you begin, it will be easier to develop them as you create the life you want.

If I were coaching you right now, I would ask you if you are ready to make the Big Change that will lead to authenticity in your life. Are you? Are you truly committed, or is it a fake commitment?

If your answer is that you are ready to make a whole-hearted commitment, then I request that you write "courage, commitment, clarity, and compassion" on some sticky notes and place them in several very visible places at home and at work. This will help you remember the four Cs as you tackle your Big Change and create a meaningful life.

If your answer is that you are not yet ready to make the Big Change, read on. I know that you will become ready as you apply the practical wisdom that lies in the pages ahead.

Chapter 2

Just How Conscious Are You?

If we lack emotional intelligence whenever stress rises the human brain switches to autopilot and has an inherent tendency to do more of the same, only harder. Which, more often than not, is precisely the wrong approach in today's world.—

Dr. Robert K. Cooper, *Executive EQ: Emotional Intelligence in Leadership and Organizations*

Oh no—this looks like another book with six million concepts to master and a long list of things to do! I want something that is practical and easy to understand. Come on, Frank—please don't be like all the other authors. I want change, not more to do's. If this is what you are thinking right now, relax. This book contains what my wife refers to as *practical wisdom*. Practical wisdom is wisdom you can use in your everyday life without having to constantly go back to the book to refresh what the terms mean. It is knowledge that produces results. The practical wisdom I present here will guide seekers to a meaningful life.

Don't let your fears from the past get in the way of seeing new possibilities in this material. Our fears act as blinders that permit us to see only things that we have experienced before. The blinders cause us to function in an **unconscious** manner. We wander around, reacting to current crises by shutting down our senses to everything but the seemingly unrelenting problem before us. (Right here, if I were one of those other authors, I would explain where in your brain all of this is taking place.

Who cares! We just want to come up with a wonderful solution to our current dilemmas.)

A meaningful life requires that you see possibilities in your life where before you only experienced fear. A meaningful life requires you to live in the present moment. When people start my Change Your Energy—Change Your Life teleclass, they know what present-moment living is and they want more of it. The question is, how do you find it?

In *Man's Search for Meaning*, Viktor Frankl describes how a meaningful life lived in the present moment is found. He wrote: "Between stimulus and response, there is a space. In that space lays our freedom and power to choose our response. In our response lies our growth and freedom."

In the gap between stimulus and response, you will find the meaningful life and all of the possibilities you seek.

It is in our ability to create a gap between stimulus and response that a meaningful life resides. It was Frankl's ability to create the gap that enabled him to survive the horrors of a concentration camp. He knew that his mission was to tell the story of what happened in the death camps so that it would never happen again. So no matter what his captors did to him (stimulus), he directed his brain to create a gap long enough to remember his mission and then respond in a way that would allow him to continue living so that he could tell his story. He was able to find meaning where others found none.

I believe that creating a meaningful life is directly correlated to your ability to create the gap between stimulus and response. It is within the gap that you make decisions about how you will live your life. It is within the gap that you decide if you want to experience the power of love and joy or feel the limitation that fear produces. It is within the gap that you determine the magnitude of the possibilities that exist in your life. The size of the gap is completely under your management; you just haven't figured that out yet.

Let me illustrate this concept for you. The basic premise that a gap exists between stimulus and response is depicted below.

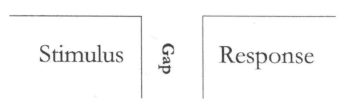

This is a simple yet incredibly important concept to master.

Your life is the result of the choices you make. It is within the gap that you make all of the choices for your life. To have a joy-filled life in which you experience all that the universe has to offer, you must be able to create a gap between stimulus and response where you can see multiple outcomes to a situation and select the one that is in alignment with your mission in life.

Unfortunately, too often there is little or no gap between stimulus and response. We just keep making the same fear-based choices we always make and end up living our lives unconsciously, without purpose

The graphic below illustrates what it looks like when there is little or no gap between stimulus and response.

Stimulus | Response

When there is no gap, people often feel that there are few or no possibilities for their lives. It is fear that causes the gap between stimulus and response to shrink. When there is no gap, you can't see alternatives in the situation you are facing. Black and white thinking occurs. Your blinders have built up throughout your life and are severely limiting your vision.

At best, the lack of a gap produces a boring, uninspiring life with little or no joy. The worst outcome is that hope begins to disappear. Hope that your life will ever improve vanishes. When hope disappears, depression is not far behind. If you find yourself having the same discussion over and over again with someone and the end result is that you both walk away unhappy, that is an example of not having a gap between stimulus and response. Replay the discussion in your mind and see if you don't repeat the same pattern each time you have it. One person says something that is perceived as an attack, to which the aggrieved responds with his or her standard response, and around it goes. There is no gap. Neither party sees any other possible way to approach the subject. Fear emerges for both of the combatants, and each says, "My way is right." When we find ourselves doing or saying things that are out of line with who we want to be, I can assure you there is no gap.

Life doesn't have to operate that way. When there is no gap, life is a struggle. Anxiety becomes the normal feeling that surges through you. Early on, we learn how we should respond to all of the stimuli in life. We learn whether we should respond with fear or joy to everything we experience. Then, for the rest of our lives, we repeat the same response patterns over and over again unless we decide to examine those patterns and perhaps respond in a different way. When we experience fear instead of responding to stimulus in a way that generates possibilities, we end up reacting without thought and desiring to control what is happening.

Stimulus   React

Where there is no gap between stimulus and response, there is no ability to live in the present moment. Fear causes us to live in the past and project that onto the future.

It is in that fear-constricted gap between stimulus and reaction where we judge or criticize ourselves and others. Constantly judging our own thoughts and actions, as well as the thoughts and actions of others, is the source of a lot of stress in our lives. Judgments can change interactions that should be enjoyable into defensive communications and even conflicts. If you are in automatic reaction mode, you will find it difficult to be a great listener. Instead of listening, you are formulating what you will say next.

Here is a simple test to see how often there is no gap for you. Simply notice how many times in a day you say, "Yes, but . . ." Every time you say this, you are projecting the past into the present and worrying about the future outcome. Fear has taken hold when you say any form of "Yes, but . . ." You are defending your fears from the past. This phrase is a clue to your partner in the conversation you are having that it is her turn to defend her statement. Conversations always go downhill when "yes, but . . ." is used. Some other forms of this phrase include the following:

- I have always done it that way.
- I can't because . . . (fill in the blank).
- I don't know how to . . . (fill in the blank).
- You don't understand my situation.
- I'll try to . . . (fill in the blank).

A friend of mine shared a phrase that I now frequently use with my coaching clients who are giving me a fear-based reason for not doing something. The phrase is, "There are either reasons or results." Reasons are the fears that eliminate the gap between stimulus and response. What is the favorite reason you give to others for not doing something? What is your reason for not living the life of your dreams?

If you want to live in the present and experience joy and abundance, reacting is not the way to do it. When you react, you are allowing the past to dictate what is happening now.

To experience all that the Divine has in store for you, you must learn to expand the gap between stimulus and response. It is within the gap between stimulus and response that all the possibilities for your life exist.

The laws of physics tell us that expansion requires increasing the amount of energy applied to a situation. The emotions of love and fear are measures of the amount of energy we are emitting. Love is a more powerful energy than fear. By learning to consistently experience love, you can provide the energy needed to expand the gap between stimulus and response.

Our mental and emotional diets determine our overall energy levels, health, and well-being to a far greater extent than most people realize. Every thought and feeling, no matter how big or small, impacts our inner energy reserves.—Doc Childre and Howard Martin, *The HeartMath Solution*

In order to experience freedom and growth as Viktor Fankl suggests, you must be capable of experiencing love and joy in the gap between stimulus and response.

When you create the gap between stimulus and response, you are living in the present. Your life is no longer controlled by fear-based response patterns from the past. Enlarging the gap can mean expanding it by a nanosecond, a minute, an hour, or longer. It is not important how large the gap is, only that you create one.

In my Change Your Energy—Change Your Life teleclass, I always discuss stimulus, gap, and response in the first session. At the end of the session, I request that the participants focus on creating a gap during the two-week intersession between the classes. The second session begins with a review of how they did. The following are a few of the successes clients have had over the years with creating a gap.

Helen had a difficult time speaking her opinion when she disagreed with what someone else said, especially with her boyfriend of several years. She would keep her mouth shut but continue to process the event for a long time afterward, all the while getting more upset about not saying anything. As a result of the class, she chose to create a gap and not take the person's comments personally, realizing that was just his or her opinion. She stopped replaying disquieting conversations over again in her mind. Life quickly became calmer. Later on we worked on expressing her opinion instead of just being quiet.

During the intersession between teleclasses, Joe found himself having the same argument he always had with his wife. Every time they discussed a particular topic, they both said the same things, had the same feelings, and nothing ever got resolved. This time, midway through the argument, Joe decided to create a gap and stop the argument. He informed his wife that they were going over the same ground they had trod before, and he needed a break. He requested that they continue the discussion later. The next morning, he resumed the conversation. By now Joe had considered some other options and recognized the fears that the heated discussion had brought out in him. They were finally able to see things differently and resolve the issue.

Susie volunteers at a kindergarten. Somehow there was a mix-up one day when she was asked to be at the school to help with registering kids for next year. No one showed up. In the past Susie would have sat at the school fuming about the incompetence, getting increasingly more upset about wasting her time and the school's money. Instead she focused on the assignment of creating a gap and managing her emotions. She went around the school asking people if they needed any assistance. That afternoon she went home feeling great about herself because of the choice she had made and how she had really helped several teachers.

Here is some practical wisdom for you. Write these words on a sticky note: **Stimulus, Gap,** and **Response**.

Place the note in several places as a reminder of what you want to do. Then begin to look for instances in your life where there is no gap between stimulus and response. Look for places where on some level fear is taking over and causing you to react. Decide to create a gap.

- Decide to create a gap where you focus on what someone is saying to you instead of multitasking.
- Decide to create a gap by not responding harshly to a question just because you are tired and have low energy.

- Decide to create a gap when your fear gets in the way and stops you from fully engaging in something you know you want to do. Use the gap to find a way forward.
- Decide to create a gap and develop a creative solution to a problem that in the past would have caused you hours worth of worrying.
- Decide to create a gap and respond in a peaceful way the next time your airline flight is severely delayed.

Several years ago, when a client did this she realized that there were too many occasions when she was "reacting" to her daughters. She was not creating a gap so that she could respond in love instead of reacting from fear. Too often she found herself giving short, uncaring responses to her daughters. She wasn't taking the time to look at them when they asked questions. She considered herself good at multitasking, so she would respond to them while continuing to do something else. That wasn't the kind of mother she wanted to be. Her kids are very important to her, and she wanted to give them her full attention. She wanted to change. Her clever idea was to explain the stimulus, gap, response process to them and give them permission to say, "Mom, remember the gap" whenever they heard her reacting. It worked beautifully, and the client began creating a gap between stimulus and response that dramatically reduced the tension in the house. When she heard them say, "Mom, gap," she would pause, take a deep breath, and focus her attention on them, showering them with the kind of love that matched who she is.

The ego doesn't disappear when you create a gap. When there is no gap between stimulus and response, the fear-fueled ego works at **E**dging **G**od **O**ut. As love/joy fills the gap, the focus of the ego is now on **E**ngaging **G**od's **O**pportunities.

Earlier I listed the following phrases as clues that you are allowing the past to dictate your current situation:

- Yes, but . . .
- I have always done it that way.
- I can't because . . . (fill in the blank).
- I don't know how to . . . (fill in the blank).
- You don't understand my situation.
- I'll try to . . . (fill in the blank).

These are all responses that indicate that fear is operating in the gap, and your response is limiting what you experience in your life. Decide which of these or similar phrases you use to keep yourself stuck, and then notice how often you say it. When you find yourself wanting to say:

- *Yes, but* . . . as an excuse for why you didn't do something, stop, admit that it is not done, and make whatever plans you need to make to complete the task.
- *I have always done it that way,* stop and determine if you want to defend old behavior or explore new alternatives.
- *I can't,* stop and decide if you really can't because you don't have the ability or if you can't because an old fear-based life pattern is stopping you.
- *I don't know how to,* stop and do the same thing you did when you said I can't.
- *You don't understand my situation,* stop and realize that you are making an excuse. Then ask yourself if you want to change your situation or remain stuck in the past. If you want to change, then seek further information on how you can move forward.
- *I'll try,* stop and realize how you are leaving the back door open for not giving it your best effort. Try is an insidious word that separates us from living a meaningful life. Either say "I will" or "I won't." Make a commitment. Don't use "I'll try" as an excuse for not going all out. When you make a committed response, you'll notice how the energy shifts to a higher level. The phrase "I'll try" cannot be part of a meaningful life in which you fully use all of your talents.

Living a meaningful life requires that you develop your capacity to expand the gap and live in the present. To live in the present, it is important to minimize the need to control people, places, and things in our lives. One of the best ways I have found to reduce my need for control and to expand the gap is to recite the Serenity Prayer, by Reinhold Niebuhr:

God grant me the serenity to accept the things I cannot change; the Courage to change the things I can; and the wisdom to know the difference. Living one day at a time; enjoying one moment at a time.

To consistently increase the gap, it is vital that you accept that there are things you can't change. As you do this, you will develop the courage to change the things you can and do it in a loving way. Mastering the stimulus, gap, response concept will dramatically change your life. If this is the only thing you remember and do from this book, the return on your investment will be huge.

Chapter 3

Here Is a Word You Won't Find in Wikipedia: Gapability

Learning to recognize when there is a small or no gap between stimulus and response is the first step toward living a conscious life in which you intentionally choose what you want to manifest. The second step is to make the decision to increase the gap, see more possibilities, and fulfill your potential.

I have created a new word to describe this concept: Gapability. Gapability is defined as your ability to create and sustain the joy that occurs when you expand the gap between stimulus and response.

I suggest using a ten-point scale to evaluate your Gapability Index. A 1 on the scale indicates little or no ability to create a gap. Fears of various kinds are likely a frequent part of your life. A 10 on the scale indicates that you are able to consistently create a gap and discover possibilities where most people see none.

Gapability Chart

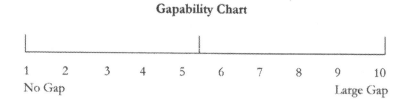

| 1 | 2 | 3 | 4 | 5 | 6 | 7 | 8 | 9 | 10 |
| No Gap | | | | | | | | | Large Gap |

If you are like most people, right now you are wondering where the in-depth assessment is to determine your Gapability. Instead, I have two questions that will assist in your self-analysis on Gapability. Gapability is not something that is definitive. It is all relative to what you want out of life.

The two questions you can use to gauge your Gapability Index are:

How often is there an ache inside that won't go away? If the answer is frequently, then your Gapability is probably a 5 or below.

How often is there a delightful buzz of wonderful energy present inside of you? If the answer is often, then you are probably a 6 or higher on the scale.

The difference between 1 and 5 and 6 and 10 is energy. If your Gapability is 5 or below, you are experiencing the energy of fear at least 51 percent of the time. When you have a Gapability score of 6 to 10, you are generating the energy of love at least 51 percent of the time.

Circle your number on the chart to indicate what you think your ability is to create a gap between stimulus and response and then fill in the information below.

Today is _____ and my Gapability Index is _____

Once you have established your current Gapability Index score, please write in the space below what you would like it to be by the time you finish reading this book.

I want my Gapability to be _____.

One tactic people use for attaining a goal is to measure their progress every day. For example, some people weigh themselves every day and others take their blood pressure every day. What if you measured your Gapability Index every day for a week? By elevating your awareness of the gap, you will see possibilities that you may have missed before. You will also realize how often the gap is reduced because of fear.

Keep track of your Gapability Index on the chart below for one week. After you fill in a number from 1 thru 10 in the blank space, write out what you noticed that day as you became more aware of your Gapability.

Day 1: My Gapability is ___
Today I noticed that _____

Day 2: My Gapability is ___
Today I noticed that _____

Day 3: My Gapability is ___
Today I noticed that _____

Day 4: My Gapability is ___
Today I noticed that _____

Day 5: My Gapability is ___
Today I noticed that _____

Day 6: My Gapability is ___
Today I noticed that _____

Day 7: My Gapability is ___
Today I noticed that _____

During the week in which you tracked your Gapability, what did you discover about your ability to sustain the joy that occurs from expanding the gap between stimulus and response? Was there a pattern to the things you noticed as you increased the gap?

When you focus on your Gapability, you are increasing your power to live a conscious life in the present. Contrast that to a life dominated by fears from the past in which there is no gap between stimulus and reaction. With a gap there is room for **creation**. When there is no gap there is only **reaction**. The words **creation** and **reaction** contain the same letters. The difference in the two is how you "c" things. Focus on creating a gap and you will see life differently.

Regardless of what your current Gapability is, my hope is that it will be higher when you finish this book and are regularly using the tools you will learn.

Early in life, you learn patterns of thinking, feeling, and acting that determine your Gapability. It is your subconscious thought patterns and emotions that determine the size of the gap. By learning to form life-controlling patterns that are centered on the emotions and thoughts that are consistent with who you were sent here to be, you will increase your Gapability. The first step in consciously creating a meaningful life is to create a gap between stimulus and response.

As we are liberated from our own fear, our presence automatically liberates others.—Marianne Williamson

Chapter 4

Do You Really Know the Truth?

Once we accept the perceptions of others as "truths," their perceptions become hardwired into our own brains, becoming our "truths."—Bruce Lipton, *The Biology of Beliefs*

As soon as I heard Colin's voice on our coaching call, I could sense that he was upset about something. He was so anxious to talk that I barely had a chance to say hello before Colin said, "I am not sure I will ever have a normal relationship with a woman. Jan and I go up and down, and we just had another stupid fight. We have been together for a year now, and disagreements just seem to pop up out of nowhere. For example, we were at a party last weekend and Jan said she overheard me tell the hostess that she was gorgeous. She thought I was flirting with the hostess. Nonsense! I was telling her what I thought about her redecorating of the house. No matter what I said, she wouldn't believe me. Eventually I just withdrew and stopped talking to her. She is always unexpectedly getting upset about something." Colin went on this way for several minutes. He thought he had limited abilities when it came to relationships. He believed that was the truth.

As we talked over the next twenty minutes, I discovered it was not a relationship problem that was causing all of his angst; it was a life-controlling pattern he had learned a long time ago that kept replaying itself. Colin's father was prone to unexpectedly getting upset and would start verbally attacking whoever was around. Colin's learned method of handling this situation was to retreat, get out of the way, and stay away until he was sure his father had calmed down. At age forty-six, Colin continued to handle unexpected disagreements the same way he did as a youngster.

The truth is he is very good at solving problems and creating lasting connections with the people he loves. It was just in this one area—unexpected upsets—that his life-controlling pattern interrupted everything and he unconsciously switched onto autopilot. He would withdraw and get angry.

I suggested that the first thing Colin and Jan could do was put a gap between stimulus and response when unexpected upsets occurred. They needed to recognize what was happening and allow themselves to stand back to observe what transpired.

Then I asked him if he wanted to end the life-controlling pattern. I explained that if he didn't create a new life-controlling pattern that more accurately reflected who he really was, he would have a difficult time staying with Jan. Colin's answer was a resounding yes He wanted to live his own truth, not his father's truth. Colin was ready to fully commit to changing this life-controlling pattern. Since then, he has developed a life pattern that allows him to create a gap between stimulus and response, and he is able to calmly discuss the issues when unexpected disputes occur.

Stop! I am not suggesting that you blame everything that is troublesome in your life on your parents. Virtually invisible life-controlling patterns that are based on fears learned from others are the biggest barrier to people living to their full potential and a meaningful life. For that reason I am sharing with you practical wisdom on how to recognize negative life-controlling patterns. Once you have learned to recognize them, I will describe how you can create positive life-controlling patterns that perfectly match with who you truly are. You will learn to recognize what is true for you and create a reality to match it.

As you know by now, living a meaningful life begins with putting a gap between stimulus and response. The challenge is that your conscious mind gets distracted by other events in your world. The minute your conscious mind is diverted from creating a gap, your subconscious takes over. When the subconscious identifies a situation in which it sees a risk, fear emerges and the gap immediately shrinks. The subconscious triggers the preprogrammed response, whether or not that response corresponds to the meaningful life you want to create. Since your conscious mind can be easily distracted and has infinitely less power to process information than your subconscious mind, you must become the master of what is happening in your subconscious if you want to create lasting change.

The life-controlling patterns that guide our lives are the result of what others taught us to believe life should be. Through frequent repetition, along with powerful feedback, you have learned how to act in a specific way to the events in your life. Eventually these patterns become so ingrained that we don't even recognize that they are operating, just as Colin didn't realize he was reacting to Jan the same way he had learned to react to his father's outbursts.

As you internalize these views, your ability to distinguish your real truths from what someone else says your truths should be begins to diminish. Ultimately you end up living someone else's life.

Life-controlling patterns determine how big the gap between stimulus and response is and what emotion is in the gap. Life-controlling patterns determine what choices you make in life.

Creating a meaningful life requires you to become aware of the specific life-controlling patterns that determine how you respond to the events of your life.

Let's pause for a minute while I ask you a few questions that are vital to answer before you go any further. Please write the answers to these questions in the book. This assignment is harder than it seems. I am asking you to stop and think about your life in an introspective way. This is not just for those individuals who are struggling right now; it is for everyone who wants to take his or her life to a higher level of creativity and engagement (even if you already have a seven figure bank account). As you answer these questions, you will be placing yourself in a learning mode that will enable you to get the most out of what comes next.

The questions are:

1. How does unconsciously making choices that limit the use of your talents affect the quality of your life? Think about the last time you said, "I'll try" when someone asked you to do something. Did you put in your best effort, or did you approach the task half-heartedly? Did you make excuses for why the outcome wasn't great?

2. If you decided to take charge of the choice-making process, what would you change first? Think back to a time when you

answered a question with "I don't care." What would you have done differently if you said what you really wanted to do?

3. How would your life change if you decided not to make choices that were based on an unconscious fear that you learned from someone else? Make a list of the things you would love to do but never say out loud because you are afraid of being criticized. Then next to each item, list what would change if you did them.

4. What would you do with the rest of our life if you could make choices based on abundance and joy and your ability to create? Before you answer this, I suggest that you define what abundance means to you. Now make a list of the things that bring real joy to your heart.

5. Are you ready to install life-controlling patterns of your own in your subconscious as opposed to living and experiencing the world through patterns someone else gave you? If your answer is no, ask yourself what steps you need to take to get ready.

Becoming the author of your own success story requires that you create your own set of life-controlling patterns in all the areas of your life, such as family, community, wellness, finances, relationships, and environment. Your ability to create joy and abundance is directly proportionate to your ability to create a gap between stimulus and response, which you then fill with life-controlling patterns that match your talents. In order to live the life of your dreams and "tune your soul," you must create life patterns that support who you were sent here to be.

What I have found is that most people don't even know that they have these ingrained negative life-controlling patterns. However, the patterns take up residence inside our subconscious and function as the lens through which we see the events of the world. Through them, we take action based on what we *think* we see and not necessarily the reality of a situation.

Understanding how life-controlling patterns work and beginning to recognize them is the next step in revealing the masterpiece that is you.

Life-controlling patterns have five distinct elements: Input, Thoughts (conscious and subconscious), Emotions, Actions, and Results.

Five Step Life Pattern Model

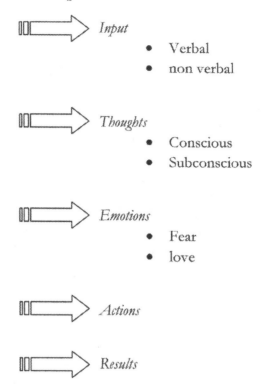

Input
- Verbal
- non verbal

Thoughts
- Conscious
- Subconscious

Emotions
- Fear
- love

Actions

Results

From the day of your birth, society imposed upon you its fixed description of the world. Society said it was a world where you must fight, where you must be liked and accepted, and so on. Through thought and speech and action you repeated this description until it hardened into the only world you knew. You were then stuck with this illusory and punishing world. Cease to repeat the description. That will make the false world fall away, to reveal the real.—Vernon Howard, *There is a Way Out*

How the Five Elements Operate

As you read this description of how each of the five parts of a life-controlling pattern work, think of an automatic response you consistently have to something that is said to you or an event that happens in your presence. Notice if your reaction tracks with what is being described here.

Input

Your mind is constantly receiving input. The input is coming from many different sources. It can be either verbal or nonverbal. It can be directed at you, or you may just be observing the event. Input can be anything that your five senses detect in your surroundings.

From birth through age two, children take in vast amounts of input as they learn to survive. Some of the input is given directly to the child, while other input is the result of what the child observes in his or her surroundings. Parents know that they are teaching when they say to their two-year-old child, "Pick up your toys." However, parents are seldom aware of how often they are providing input (or teaching) when they are not speaking directly to their children. For example, Mom and Dad are teaching when they are kind and loving toward each other in the presence of their child. While observing his parents, the child learns that is okay to demonstrate love toward a spouse. If Mom and Dad never touch, hug, or say loving things to each other, then the child learns not to express love openly. Notice that in both examples, the parents did not have to say one word about how to demonstrate love. The child observes it, learns it, stores it, and replays it throughout his lifetime.

Going back to my client Colin—he received input from his father that emotional outbursts from family members/loved ones can occur unexpectedly at any time. He was never safe as a kid from experiencing outbursts that upset him.

Thoughts

The input you receive is taken into the conscious mind. The conscious mind makes a decision to accept or reject the input. If the conscious mind accepts the input, it gets passed onto the subconscious. Whatever the conscious mind says yes to, the subconscious mind must accept. The power of what is stored in the subconscious to impact your life is a function of how often you received certain input, the influence the source of the input had on you, and/or the sheer magnitude of the event. As a result of the repetition and/or intensity of input, patterns or models for how we will feel and the action we take in the future are created and stored in the subconscious.

When we are born, we have a hundred billion brain cells, and only a small percentage of them are connected. During the first three years of life, each brain cell creates over 15,000 connections. The brain creates intricate pathways through which information is communicated and stored. These synaptic connections are created so that the brain can instantly recognize what is happening and make determinations about our safety.

Through synaptic connections of one brain cell to another, our behavior is literally hard-wired into us. To change behavior, we need to create new synaptic connections. You must repeat the same input over and over again with an emotional intensity that causes a new connection to occur. This is the reason change is so difficult. It is also why they say it takes twenty-one days to break a habit and create a new one. You literally have to rewire your brain.

This concept of creating synaptic connections early in our development points out the power others have on imprinting in a child what he or she thinks about life. The life patterns we have are generally the result of input we have received from other people during the first two to three years of our lives.

Let me repeat that again: our life-controlling patterns were formed during the first two to three years of our lives.

Unfortunately, most adults teach children behaviors that are pleasing to the adults. What children are taught seldom has any connection to the child's talents. To compound this even further, the adults are teaching from life patterns that operate at the subconscious level. The adults are often unaware of what they are teaching their children. This is especially true of the adults' nonverbal actions and behaviors, which are observed and absorbed by the kids.

When mystics and spiritual teachers talk about being unconscious in your approach to life, they are describing people who are living a life driven by subconscious life patterns installed in your subconscious by others. You are unaware of what you are doing, and your actions were programmed into you without your permission. Your mind and your body are on automatic pilot. To be conscious in your approach to life is to choose your own life-controlling patterns and create ones that match the *uniqueness* the Divine placed in you.

Now here's another surprise. As the subconscious learns to recognize the input it receives, it also learns the appropriate emotion that accompanies the input. The brain recognizes the input and learns how to feel about it. That leads us to the next part of life patterns—emotions.

Before we move on, let's go back to Colin again. His girlfriend Jan had unexpectedly gotten angry at him because he was talking to another woman. His response was to withdraw and stop talking. Because of the power and repetition of his father's outbursts when Colin was a youngster, Colin had created a very vivid picture in his subconscious. Decades later he easily remembered how fearful he was of those unexpected outbursts. His subconscious was always on the lookout for those unsafe times. He learned to attach the emotion of fear to unexpected emotional outbursts expressed by anyone.

Emotion

The dictionary says that emotion is part of the conscious mind that involves feeling. I have created another definition that I would like to share:

Emotion is our internal measure of the completeness of the connection we feel with Self, others, and the Divine.

I believe there are two basic emotions: love/joy and fear. Love is when we feel fully connected to our Self, others, and the Divine. Fear exists when there is some level of disconnection between Self, others, and the Divine.

Fear is the emotion that gets associated with many thought patterns that are stored in the synapses of the brain. You can easily understand fear is the predominant emotion for many people if you look at how we teach children to live in this world. We most often teach children by telling them what not to do. Make a list right now of all the things you tell or told your children not to do when they were infants and toddlers.

Here are some examples of what people put on their lists as ways to discourage certain behaviors: don't color outside the lines, don't talk unless you are spoken to, don't touch—that is fragile, don't cause trouble, don't cry/boys don't cry, don't play with toys in the dirt, and nice girls don't do that.

Whenever we learn *not* to do something, we are normally installing a fear that is hoped to prevent the action from happening again.

Our brains are like computers that have been programmed by someone else to meet their needs, not ours. And the program is always running in the recesses of our subconscious minds, dictating how to respond to the events we encounter. As the invisible patterns that are based on fears run, they suck the energy right out of us and slow us down—the same way a virus does in a computer. If you want a different outcome in your life, you must create and store a new program/life-controlling pattern in the subconscious that is not rooted in fear.

Our emotions, just like our thought patterns, become hard-wired in our brains. A neural pathway has been created that enables you to recognize an object or situation and then automatically generate the emotion that goes along with it.

Thoughts do not determine the action, emotions do. For Colin, it was the fear he learned that caused his reaction, which was the desire to hide and end the relationship.

Action

Emotion is the energy that produces an action by our bodies. The action could be as simple as a raised eyebrow, or it could be much more physical, such as hugging to demonstrate our love for the other person. Of course, there is as wide of an array of actions as there are people to think them up.

What is important for our purposes is to remember that the action will be the outcome of the emotion.

Actions fall into one of two broad categories: they are loving/creative and expanding energy, or they are fearful and contracting energy.

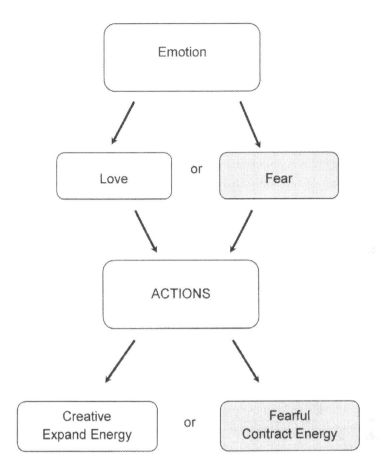

The action we take will be the one that is intended to produce a result that will reinforce the pattern we have stored in our subconscious. Colin learned to retreat and not say anything so that he would not be the recipient of any more anger.

If you want to change your life, you must change your actions. In order to change your actions, you must first change the emotion that is automatically created when you receive input.

If you feel love/joy, you will take one kind of action, and if you feel fear then you will take another kind of action. This is an incredibly powerful concept that has massive impact on the way we live.

Colin agreed that he wanted to recognize what was happening and change his actions so that he didn't prematurely end a wonderful relationship because he was fearful of Jan's emotion.

Result

Of course all of our actions produce a result. Our brains process the result to determine if it matches the results we have stored about similar events. If it matches, it further reinforces what we did. If it does not match, we normally do the same thing over again harder, louder, softer, or some other variation on the same theme in an attempt to produce the result we desire.

We don't question whether the actions we are taking can actually produce the desired result. We have stored in our minds what the result should be, and we are going to achieve it. So we keep repeating the same actions over and over again in an attempt to produce a result that will never come. No matter how often you add one plus one, you will never get three. No matter how often you stop talking and hide when there is conflict, you will not create loving, wonderful relationships in your life. This is the definition of insanity—doing the same thing over again and expecting different results. However, it is not really insanity; we are literally hard-wired to act this way.

What became obvious to me as I studied this process was that the gap between stimulus and response was the result of my ability to manage not just my thoughts, but also my emotions. When I learned to recognize the emotion, I was able to expand the gap, see more possibilities in situations, and then take an action that would lead to my preferred outcome.

The challenge in life is not to be a positive thinker. The challenge is to become aware of our life patterns and create ones that are in alignment with our talents while disregarding those that are out of sync with our souls. We need to learn to recognize and manage our emotions. The challenge is to choose and create positive emotions.

Life-controlling patterns become our identity. We will do everything we can to protect our identities as we perceive them. If you want to change your identity, you must learn to manage your emotions. You must learn to feel love and joy no matter what is happening around you. This is not about putting on rose-colored glasses and ignoring what is taking place around you. It is about developing the courage and faith to create what you want despite what takes place around you.

Let me give you another example of a life pattern and how it gets formed. Mary was a coaching client who as a youngster was constantly given the message from her parents, both verbally and nonverbally, that hard work pays off and you shouldn't waste time. You can play after the work is done and oh, by the way, work is never done. Hard work and concentration are the keys to success in the viciously competitive corporate world in which both her parents struggled every day. She learned the lesson that unless you work relentlessly, you will be a failure in life.

As you might suspect, Mary became a workaholic. She was totally unfamiliar with the concept of having joy and fun in her life. She felt that she only had value in the world when she was engaged in some productive activity.

The life pattern works like this:

Input: By the time Mary is two years old, she has heard and/ or observed from both parents that hard work and getting the job done are the keys to success in life. Fun only happens after the work's done, and the work is never done.

Thought stored in the subconscious: In her subconscious, Mary has the thought that there is no time for fun. She must always be productive or she will be useless.

Emotion: Fear is the emotion that is attached to the thought. When she is done with one thing, she immediately looks for something else to do. In her early years, she learned that if she wasn't busy doing what her father considered being productive, she would be criticized and/or given a task to do.

Action: As an adult, Mary finds a job that is highly structured and dives into it, allowing it to consume all of her waking (and sometimes non-waking) hours. She fears that she must always receive a performance review that is outstanding. If not, she might be fired.

Result: Mary never really feels any joy in her job, regardless of how often she is promoted. She works nonstop and has high blood pressure. She never has time to have any fun. As a matter of fact, she doesn't know how to have fun. Her kids have grown up, and she doesn't even realize what she missed.

She just did what she was taught. Mary was not defective; she was just living the life that was programmed inside of her.

Mary loves to draw, and her heart was aching to do more with her real talent. However, she learned that art was not a productive activity. After some coaching, she is now finding time to draw and she loves it. Sound familiar?

Life-controlling patterns are like atomic-powered submarines—they run silent, long, and deep. We aren't aware of their presence, yet they are always affecting what we do, from earning money to raising kids.

Physiologically it simply doesn't matter whether your anger is justified or not. The body doesn't make moral judgments about feelings; it just responds.—Doc Childre and Howard Martin, *The HeartMath Solution*

Chapter 5

The Invisible Force: Emotions

Don't forget that little emotions are the great captains of our lives.—Vincent van Gogh

The positive thinking gurus are wrong! They tell you that changing your life is the result of changing your thoughts. That notion is inaccurate and incomplete.

It disregards the fact that when your subconscious was programmed decades ago to recognize the stimulus, it was also programmed to attach a specific emotion to that thought pattern. The emotion is generated almost simultaneously to the thought. Change won't occur until you alter the emotion that is attached to the thought. You can think over and over again, "I am a millionaire." That won't lead you to becoming a millionaire. It ignores the emotion that goes with the thought. I ask my coaching clients to think the statement "I am a millionaire" and notice what emotion emerges inside. Invariably what they report is the emotion of fear. Their fear of being a bad person, too old, too dumb, too poor, too short, too female, too young, or too inexperienced comes to the surface. Sure, you might be excited when you first have the thought of being a millionaire, but what happens within seconds of being excited about the abundance? Your fear, whatever it may be, of why that is not possible for you begins to takeover.

Try it for yourself and see what happens. The basic feeling people have is that money is bad, and that people who have lots of it have done something wrong to get it. Unless you change the emotion that goes with the thought, nothing will change. Every time you receive input about money and think about being a millionaire, your subconscious will always go to the emotion that was originally programmed until you consciously change the emotion. So when you think a thousand times, "I am a millionaire" and your fear is still in place, you reinforce the idea that it will never happen. Is that what you want?

Changing the emotion is the key. Go back to my life-controlling pattern model and notice the flow. Action follows emotion, not thoughts. Thoughts don't produce actions. Thoughts without emotion are daydreams. In order to change your life, you must change your pattern of emotions. When you change your emotions, you change your energy, and when you change your energy, you change your life. The power of emotion in changing your life has been given little if any recognition by most positive-thinking gurus.

One the most read self-development gurus, Napoleon Hill, didn't overlook emotion. What many people remember about Napoleon Hill's great book *Think and Grow Rich* is how often he writes about focusing your thoughts. They forget that every time he writes about the power of thought he adds that thought must be charged by positive emotion. If you're not familiar with Hill's work, find a copy of the book and check for yourself. A better title for the book would have been *Emote and Grow Rich*.

Emotion or the lack of it is always present in our lives. If you pay close attention to the words people use and the energy they put behind them, you will notice how often the emotion of fear is limiting full engagement with life.

During a recent conference call with several of my colleagues, we were discussing a white paper one of the call participants had written. The white paper was an important element in Susan's development of a web-based marketing campaign for her coaching services. She had done some editing since the last time we had seen it, and it was very well done. However, Susan's description of the paper was "I have done some work on it and it is okay." Her comment lacked a sense of enthusiasm for what she had written. I inquired as to why she was withholding her excitement for what she had written. She responded, "As a kid I was always bubbling over with energy and excited about everything. However, my dad did not share my enthusiasm and told me on many occasions to settle down. Life is hard. I learned to control my enthusiasm. I can still hear his voice." The learned emotion of fear of being criticized led to the action of always holding back a wonderful joy for life that Susan possessed. After we discussed what was happening, she was able to put her wonderful energy into describing what she had written. How can you create an exciting marketing campaign if you have learned to never get excited yourself?

The Law of Attraction basically says that energy attracts to itself like energy. If Law of Attraction works, then you must change your energy to change your life. If you want to change your energy, you must change your emotions. You must shift to a higher level of emotion. The Law of Attraction is working as long as you are alive. The Law of Attraction is perpetually in operation. It doesn't just work when you are focused on it. It is always in place. If you want to attract to you anything that vibrates at a high level, then you must consistently send that same energy. Your emotions determine the energy you are sending into the field.

When you manage your emotions, you are managing the outcome of your life. In order to put the Law of Attraction to work in your life, you must consistently ask yourself, "What do I want to transmit?" Then make sure your emotion is a vibrational match to what you want to create.

It is the emotion that determines what type of action you can take, and it is the action that will determine the nature of your life. It is emotion that drives the Law of Attraction and determines what the universe mirrors back to you.

In order to live your full potential and tune your soul, you must create life-controlling patterns that support what you were sent here to be. When you change your emotion, you will change your energy, and that will change your life. That is the real "secret"!

To highlight the power of our emotions and their link to the Law of Attraction, I wrote a short statement that you can use to attract joy and abundance. It is adapted from Wallace Wattles' *The Science of Getting Rich*.

Joy and Abundance are the result of doing things in a certain way.

> *There is an energy that communicates, from which all things are made, and which in its original state permeates, penetrates, and fills the interspaces of the universe.*
>
> *I can form things with my emotion and by impressing my emotions upon formless substance can cause the thing I feel to be created.*
>
> *In order to do this, I must shift from life-controlling patterns based on fears to love-based life-controlling patterns. I must create love-based life-controlling patterns that express the essence of what I want. And I must hold these love-powered patterns in my heart with the fixed purpose to manifest my heart's desire. I will create an unwavering faith that the energy of the Divine flows through me—closing my heart to all that may tend to shake my purpose, dim my vision, or quench my faith.*
>
> *I am ready to receive joy and abundance when it comes, and I am fully connected with the people and things in my present environment through the love-based life-controlling patterns resident within me.*

If you would like to further enhance the energy that you are sending into the Universe and aid the creation of a meaningful life, I suggest you do the following exercise:

Put a smile on your face and focus your mind's eye on what you want to create in your life. Then read out loud the statement I shared entitled Joy and Abundance. *Repeat the reading several times a day. After thirty days, record what is now different about your life.*

There is more power in this exercise than you can imagine. Later in the book, when I explain the power of your smile, you will understand why this exercise is effective.

Love and fear each have a very different energy about them. The emotion of love vibrates at a much higher level than fear. When you are living your full potential, you will experience the high energy of love and reap the benefits both physically, spiritually, and mentally that arise.

The energy of fear, on the other hand, sets off lower vibrations that are detrimental to our health and well-being.

A meaningful life is a function of learning to feel and vibrate at the emotion of love more than you vibrate at fear.

Fear-Based Life-Controlling Patterns

Life-controlling patterns based on fear are the result of input we have received from others that leads us to believe if we don't act in a certain way, something negative will happen to us. If you don't behave in prescribed way, you learn that:

- you won't be loved
- you will be broke
- you will be laughed at
- you will be punished verbally or physically
- you will never find a husband/wife/partner
- you won't get into the college you want
- you won't make the team
- you will be loved less than your siblings
- you will get a poor grade
- you will be abandoned
- you won't get promoted
- God will punish you for that action
- you will be criticized for speaking out
- you will fail

For example:

Shelia learned that unless she got straight A's on her report card, her parents would withhold their love. Her fear was that if she wasn't perfect, the people whom she loved would withhold their affection.

Bill learned that unless he got a real job and gave up his desires to write novels, he would be broke. As a result, he was afraid to pursue his real passion and was very bored as an editor for a newspaper.

Sue learned that if she was too smart, none of the boys would want to date her and she would never get married. She learned to always hide her intelligence and never really gave her best on any project at work. Her fear of being too smart meant that she was relegated to jobs that were below her ability.

These are just a few of the thousands of things we can be taught by others to fear.

During teleclasses when I start to describe life-controlling patterns based on fears, participants typically think that they don't have any major fears that are stopping them from living their full potential. This is particularly true of men (sorry guys, it is true). The word fear automatically takes people to thoughts of real physical harm. Furthermore, real men and successful women don't admit to being afraid of anything. As you can see from the list above, I am seldom talking about real harm. In the vast majority of cases, the fear is of a perceived negative outcome. Notice that I wrote perceived negative outcome. The acronym for FEAR—False Expectations Appearing Real—is true. It is estimated that over 90 percent of our worries never come true. Life-controlling patterns based on fears cause you to feel defective. You are not defective; you are just doing what you unknowingly learned early in life. You are just living down to the limited potential that you learned that you had.

As I explain what I mean by fear, the teleclass participants relax and begin to realize that they do have some fears. For example, in a teleclass I did several years ago, a woman spoke up and said she wasn't aware of any fears in her life at that time. She had a great marriage, her kids were great, and her business was growing. I inquired as to what the major hurdle was that was preventing her business from growing at a faster rate. She replied that she needed to spend more time making phone calls. Sensing a life-controlling pattern there, I asked what the attitude was in her home when she was young regarding talking on the phone. She immediately replied that her mother hated talking on the phone, as did her father. She was not permitted to spend a lot of time on the phone. Bingo! There was the life-controlling pattern. She was reprimanded if she spent too much time on the phone when she was young. This life-controlling pattern was slowing the growth of her business because she was fearful of spending too much time on the phone. To spend time on the phone to meet the demands of her business, she would have to change the energy/emotion around it.

Our reactions to the result in a life-controlling pattern based on fear are interesting. Think for a moment about when you were in the middle of a life-controlling pattern based on fear—who did you blame for the result? Fear often causes us to blame others for unwanted outcomes. This allows us to operate very comfortably as victims. Blaming others is one of the behaviors that cause the gap between stimulus and result to shrink. Generating possible solutions for the challenges in life is limited when we are in the blaming-others mode.

What is really sad about being a victim is that you never really get to experience what life is like when you engage all of your talent.

With life-controlling patterns based on fear, you don't question the thought that is stored in the subconscious or the emotion that is attached to it to determine if they were appropriate in the given situation. Instead you question why someone behaved in a way that didn't give you the result that you wanted and expected. How many times have you said (or heard someone else say) that you would have gotten the result you wanted in a situation if only the other party had behaved differently? These life-controlling patterns keep us hoping that others will behave differently than they typically do. You keep asking yourself, Why can't they see it my way? Well, it's because other people have life-controlling patterns based on fear that are just as strong as yours are. They are saying to themselves, Why can't that idiot see it correctly? In order to create a meaningful life that is filled with joy and abundance, you must be able to recognize your own life-controlling patterns as well as the life-controlling patterns of others. When you can do this, you will be able, as Don Miguel Ruiz says in *The Four Agreements*, to not take things personally.

Early in life, the fears of our parents and other significant caregivers are transferred to us disguised as "the truths about how life works." Life-controlling patterns based on fear become the silent thieves that rob us of a life filled with joy and abundance. Instead of experiencing a life as if it were in 3D on an IMAX screen with digital surround sound, we experience life as a monochrome/monaural event that offers few alternatives. I know that it is possible for you to have the 3D life that uses all of your talents.

I coached a woman who, on the surface, appeared to be a positive person and enjoyed life. In reality she was a very angry person who had learned to smile to cover up how she really felt. She had been smiling for decades and had come to believe that the smile made her a joyful person. However, the anger came right to the surface when we discussed her upcoming performance review at work. Her goal was to not let the manager win. What I found out was that by "win," she meant that she would not allow the manager to put anything in her review that indicated she was not doing a great job. She was not open to any feedback. Furthermore, she had no ideas what she could do to further develop her talents at work. She was not interested in building a career at this company. She just wanted to be left alone and not receive any feedback. Does that sound like a happy woman on a spiritual path?

We have become masters of wearing masks that hide who we truly are. Our view of the world is limited by the life-controlling pattern based on fears that become the models by which we interpret the events of our lives. We feel as though we must defend our fear-based life patterns because they were programmed inside of us early on in life as the truth. We believe that we have a patent on the truth. The view we have must be defended at all costs. Control must be maintained. Life patterns become our identities.

You can easily detect when you or someone else is defending a life-controlling pattern based on fear. The clue is the word *but*. Invariably when we say or hear the word *but*, it is the beginning of a defense of the fear-based life pattern that is now in operation. Just for fun, begin to notice how often you say *but* and then notice what happens next. Pay attention to the feeling that is flowing silently through you. Is it a feeling of joy, cocreation, and letting go, or is it feeling of defense and the need for control? How often do you give reasons for not doing something instead of talking about the results you produced? At the core of why you give a reason instead of a result is a fear-based life-controlling pattern that prevents you from moving forward. Life-controlling patterns based on fears cause you to see yourself as less capable than you really are. At the soul level, you know that you have more talent than you have demonstrated so far. However, you have become so comfortable with an identity that is less than your potential that it is very difficult to gain enough momentum to make changes.

Recently I asked a woman I am coaching who is starting to build a network-marketing business if she had a plan for her business, and she began giving me reasons why she didn't. The reasons were the same ones she had given me several times before when we talked about expanding her business. Underneath the reasons was a life pattern of fear. The life pattern was so strong that it prevented her from seeing alternative solutions that would permit her to move forward to produce results. Her particular fear-based life pattern centered on a person with whom she thought she must work to build her business. This was a person whom she perceived to be unfair in his treatment of people. Because of events in her early life, she has a strong dislike for people whom she perceives to be unjust and prefers to stay far away from them. Once I pointed out the life-controlling pattern and suggested an alternative way of expanding the business that didn't include this man, she was able to become creative in building the rest of the business plan.

In the last decade or so, science has discovered a tremendous amount about the role emotions play in our lives. Researchers have found that even more than IQ, your emotional awareness and abilities to handle feelings will determine your success and happiness in all walks of life, including family relationships.
—John Gottman, PhD, *Raising an Emotionally Intelligent Child*

The new field of positive psychology that is being pioneered by such people as Martin Seligman and the late Paul Pearsall is shedding light on how prevalent the life-controlling pattern based on fears are. In his book *The Beethoven Factor*, Pearsall estimates that between 70 and 80 percent of the population operates at a low level of functioning that he describes as acedia. According to Pearsall, acedia was once considered one of the deadly sins. Acedia is the sin of living in fatigued apathy, cynicism, and general spiritual weariness. It is languishing at a level just barely above surviving.[1] Three quarters of the population is missing the experience of being fully alive. Only 20 percent of the population is enjoying life. Doesn't that dumbfound you? In this country where we have so much and so many are gainfully employed, over 75 percent are barely hanging on, with no joy in their lives.

Life-controlling patterns based on fears are dominating the lives of millions of people in this country. If this were a disease, it would have been given a name or a label. I have created a term for the condition of people whose lives are dominated by life-controlling pattern based on fears: Negative Energy Syndrome (NES). People with Negative Energy Syndrome vibrate at a low frequency of energy, which prevents them from being fully engaged with life. They are not capable of consistently sustaining the emotion of love and leading lives filled with joy and abundance. They are not enjoying the fruits of a life that fully utilizes all of their potential and talents. People with NES tend to associate with other victims. They spend their time complaining about life or gossiping about others.

Here are ten signs that indicate you may have Negative Energy Syndrome:

1. Most if not all of your problems are the result of what someone else has done to you.
2. You have been in the same job, which you dread, for more than five years.
3. You have set significant goals in major areas of your life and never follow through with the actions.
4. You say "yes, but . . ." many times a day.
5. You fired your life coach because he/she kept pushing you to do things you didn't want to deal with.
6. You feel it is important to always be in control of your environment.
7. You haven't taken a real vacation in years because there is always too much to do.
8. There have been times when an angry outburst emanates from your mouth before you can really get control of it.
9. You are convinced that making more money will make you a happier person.
10. At least once a day you make judgmental comments about others and severely judgmental comments about yourself.

It is easy for people to laugh at several of the items in this list. However, there can be serious consequences to having NES. People with NES eventually begin to feel higher and higher levels of anxiety. As anxiety begins to rise, the NES sufferer begins to lose hope for his or her life. As hope begins to fade, the probability for interpersonal conflict also increases. Angry outbursts and unacceptable behavior become more commonplace.

Eliminating life-controlling patterns based on fears is simple, but it is not easy. The cure is to expand the gap between stimulus and response.

When you do that, you can begin to make the shift to love-based life patterns.

If any of the symptoms of NES resonate with you, I suggest that you begin to keep track of how often it occurs. See if you can identify the life-controlling pattern based on fear. In order to find the source, ask yourself:

1. How did important people in my early life behave regarding _____ (fill in whatever the topic is)?
2. What would happen in my life if I didn't follow this life pattern?
3. Is this life pattern serving me?
4. What do I want to change the life pattern to?

Negative Energy Syndrome can have harmful effects on marriages as well. Individuals who have deeply ingrained life-controlling patterns based on fears can find it difficult to communicate effectively with their spouse. When both of the partners in the marriage are defending their life-controlling pattern based on their fears, the result is never pretty. Neither person is listening, neither feels heard, and they never get to the real cause of their problems. Each one believes they know the truth. Both partners wonder, Why can't she/he get it? How can he/she be so stubborn? Can't he/she recognize my way is the best way?

I have observed in my years of coaching that anytime a person is experiencing resistance to something in his or her life, the underlying cause of the resistance is a life-controlling pattern based on fear.

There are words that indicate a life-controlling pattern based on fear is in operation. These words innocuously diminish your accomplishments. I have a client who kept referring to the business that provided her with a significant income as "my tiny little business." She had a fear that she was not capable of running a large business. She couldn't understand why she couldn't make the business grow any larger. Now that she has recognized the life-controlling pattern based on fear, she is beginning to see many ways in which she could grow the business.

One of the phrases that indicate a fear-based life-pattern is in operation is, "I don't know." How often do you say "I don't know" when you are asked for an opinion? "I don't know" is an excuse that covers up a fear of not being good enough. Eventually you find yourself saying "I don't know" even when you do know.

Listen to the words you use to describe yourself and your work. Notice if you are frequently discounting your talents or level of success. When that happens, ask yourself what the fear-based life pattern is behind your self-deprecation. What would happen if you were to fully embrace your talents and utilize them to the maximum? If you did that, then you would have to change your identity. You could no longer say, "I am just the owner of a business that is stuck and won't grow." You would have to describe yourself as the owner of growing business that has potential. The implication by association is that if your business has potential, then so must you. In order to accept your potential, you must give up the identity of being incapable and the attention that gets you.

Fear-based life patterns create drama in our lives. That drama that continually operates in your subconscious drains your energy. It robs you of creativity and vitality. Life-controlling patterns based on fears cause you to focus on what you can't do and project that picture into the future. The result is you are stuck repeating the same patterns over and over again. Even when you change jobs, move to a new neighborhood, or marry a spouse, that same pattern eventually reappears. A life that is driven by life-controlling patterns based on fear is a life where the phrase, "If only I can ____, then things will change" is frequently spoken. However, the "if only" never comes true.

Roberta is a client who has a high need to control what is happening in her children's lives. She is repeating what she learned from her father, who controlled everything about her life. When she started coaching with me, Roberta said, "If only I could get my son to not be so angry all of the time, life would be much better in our house. Then I could focus on finally pursuing some of my interests." The more she attempted to control him, the more turmoil was generated in the home. The truth was she was also trying to control lots of other people in her family. What a burden it was for her. The result of the drama created by attempting to control others was that Roberta was exhausted all of the time. She complained of having no time for herself. How could she have time for herself if all of her energy and time was going into controlling/taking care of others?

By now you are probably thinking about the life patterns that are driving your life. As you do, you will have to make a choice—do you create new life patterns that are completely aligned with your talents, or do you continue to allow the life-controlling patterns based on fears that were created by someone else rule you? Will you live your own life, or someone else's? Have you developed the courage to do it? That is not one of those loaded questions you get at positive thinking seminars where you are expected to shout, "Yes, I have the courage!" It is a sincere question—do you have the courage to make the Big Change and create a truly meaningful life? You may not at this time, and that is okay. There is additional work you need to do to get ready. I believe that the practical wisdom provided in this book when learned and applied will bolster your courage and launch you forward.

As quantum physicists have discovered, once you observe something, you have changed it. Observing and being aware of your life-controlling patterns is the first step in creating alignment between your talents and how you live each day.

Chapter 6

Life Is Like a Crowded Elevator— Constrained and Out of Your Control

Imagine that you are at the elevator on the second floor of a thirty-story office building. You have pushed the button and are waiting for the next elevator so that you can go up several floors. The elevator dings as it approaches your floor and the door opens. As the door opens, you see that the elevator is already almost full. Do you:

A. Squeeze on, do not look anyone in the eye, keep your mouth shut, and immediately start to worry, hoping that you get off safely?
B. Squeeze on and begin to look around for something on which you can comment so that you can connect with all of these people you don't know?
C. Look at the one or two people in the front of the elevator and confidently tell them you'll wait for the next elevator?
D. Walk away as if you weren't waiting for an elevator in the first place?

If your answer was either A or D, you probably experienced some level of fear and asked yourself one or more of the following questions:

- What if I don't fit in?
- What if something happens because there are too many people on board?

- What if someone gets too close to me?
- What If I can't get off when I am supposed to?
- What if it takes too long to get to my floor?
- What if I speak up and offend someone?
- What if I skip this one and wait for the next one? Perhaps that won't be so full and it will be less of a risk.

In answers A and D, fear has taken over and filled the gap between stimulus and response. A life-controlling, fear-based pattern subconsciously filled the gap so quickly that you didn't even recognize it was happening. (Note: I know there are people who have deep-seated psychological fears of elevators, and I am not talking about them in this example.) The fear just showed up and took over, limiting your enjoyment of the elevator experience and your opportunity to connect with others.

How often in your life does fear just show up, just like in the crowded elevator, and limit your interactions with the world? Most of us don't really know the answer to that question. If you feel that there is more you have to contribute to the world, then it is definitely happening to you with a degree of frequency of which you are not aware. I suggest that you begin to become aware of when "the elevator effect" is happening to you. The elevator effect is that uncomfortable feeling you get when life-controlling patterns based on fear take over and cause you to live/operate at a level lower than your full potential.

If you chose answers B or C from the list above, it is an indicator that you have let go of at least some fears in your life. It is easy for the real you to show up in your life.

Figuratively speaking, we have the opportunity to step into a crowded elevator many times a day. We hope that we will safely disembark from the elevator at our destination. The door of opportunity opens and we must decide if it is an opportunity that is in alignment with our goals in life or not. If it is in alignment, we have a chance to get on and move forward. Unfortunately, too often we either reject the opportunity outright or we step into the elevator and our fear causes us to automatically shut down and reject the opportunity to create and grow. As the door closes on the elevator, our fear-based life patterns close down our abilities to live full out. We are stuck. We hope that we get out of the elevator without making a mistake, vowing to never let this happen again.

As you read the previous chapters on life-controlling patterns, I'm sure you intellectually understood what I was describing. However, uncovering them in your own life can be more difficult. They are so ingrained in you that they have become invisible to the conscious mind. They have been hard-wired deep in the neural pathways of your subconscious. You have repeated them so many times over the years that you don't realize you have an automatic response to much of the outside input you receive. The door opens, you get on, the fear takes over, and the door closes. The real you automatically goes into hiding.

Take forty-five-year-old Richard for example. By now, he has been practicing his life-controlling patterns for at least forty-three years. That is over four decades of recognizing an input in the subconscious, generating the learned emotion, and then taking some form of the learned action. In forty-three years, he is lucky if there is any gap left between stimulus and response. By now it is just stimulus and response. The emotion is attached so quickly and the action just follows literally before he can blink his eye. The neural pathways in his brain are so well ingrained that he runs on autopilot way too often. After forty-three years of experiencing the same fears over and over again, life begins to feel like a crowded elevator—constrained and out of his control.

Life-controlling patterns based on fear have many of the same effects on our lives as do crowded elevators. They cause us to worry, to feel out of control, to not easily connect with others, and to behave in ways that limit our lives. These patterns cause us not to participate in ways that add real texture and meaning to our lives. The elevator effect is a shorthand way to describe what is happening in your life when fear takes over.

Let me give you an example of where the elevator effect occurred in my life. It was the middle of November at the weekly Rotary Club luncheon. During the announcements of upcoming events, the president of the club said that he was looking for volunteers to ring the bell and collect money for the Salvation Army. Those who wanted to volunteer were asked to sign a roster that was circulating through the room. (The elevator effect went into action. The door was now open, I saw that it was crowded, and subconsciously fear began to happen inside of me) When the sheet came to me, I quickly passed it on, hoping that no one would ask me why I hadn't volunteered. (I was hoping to make myself invisible and not be noticed.) By the end of the meeting, the sign-up sheet had circulated around the entire room and no one had approached me about volunteering. (I had arrived at my destination and was getting off the elevator safe and sound.)

So the elevator door opened and I automatically selected answer A: squeeze on, do not look anyone in the eye, and keep your mouth shut while I immediately began to worry and hope that I got off safely.

However, for twenty minutes after the sign-up sheet went by, I sat there debating with myself about what the fear was and whether I should deal with it. Why had I chosen answer A? Thinking of ringing the bell brought back memories of many times in the Midwest when I saw bell-ringing volunteers standing in the freezing snowy or wet weather ringing their hearts out. I always admired them for standing there in the cold while others rushed about enjoying the holiday. As I approached them, I would always say to myself, *No way would I ever do that.*

Fortunately, the story does not stop there. I recognized the elevator effect was in full force and trying to drag me onboard. The real me wants to give back to the world, and I realized that I wanted to give answer C. I wanted to squeeze on and begin to look around for something to comment on so that I could connect with all of these people I didn't know.

I found the sheet at another table and signed up for a two-hour bell-ringing shift in front of Albertson's Grocery. I can't remember the last time I felt my hands sweat as much as they did while I was signing the sheet.

That evening during dinner, I told my wife what I had done. I threw out the idea that maybe she would like to join me for some of the shift, fully expecting her to say something about the joy of doing this on my own. To my surprise, not only did she say yes, she decided to dress up like an elf. My bell-ringing challenge suddenly wasn't feeling so bad. Maybe this could be fun. It was in fact great fun, and we raised a lot of money.

If I hadn't recognized the elevator effect and dealt with the fear, I would have missed a great day. On that day I dealt with the what-if questions and was able to say to myself, *Wow, what a great chance to interact with some new people. This could be fun.*

In order to live a meaningful life, you must develop the ability to put a gap between stimulus and response so that you recognize when you have just stepped into the elevator effect. Create a gap and decide which answer from the list you really want to give: A, B, C, or D.

A. Squeeze on, do not look anyone in the eye, keep your mouth shut and immediately start to worry, hoping that you get off safely.

B. Squeeze on and begin to look around for something on which you can comment so that you can connect with all of these people you don't know.

C. Look at the one or two people in the front of the elevator and confidently tell them you'll wait for the next elevator.

D. Walk away as if you weren't waiting for an elevator in the first place.

In the next chapter I begin sharing practical wisdom to free yourself from life-controlling patterns based on fear so that you can consciously and easily select answers B or C when the door opens on a crowded elevator.

If we could just free ourselves from our perceived limitations and tap into our internal fire, the possibilities are endless.—Dean Karnazes, author of *Ultramarathon Man*

Chapter 7

The Real Secret to a Meaningful Life

NOTE TO READER: **This is a chapter you will want to study if living a very meaningful life where you fully utilize all of your talents is important to you. I encourage you to underline words and phrases that jump out at you. Take notes on this chapter and read it several times. Casual reading of this chapter will not lead to the Big Change you desire.**

Not long ago, a client named Dan sent me this e-mail:

> *I have had a seriously profound experience today. I am in Murray teaching a seminar all day tomorrow and again on Tues. I went to what they call their exercise room here at the motel, and 2 out of the 4 machines didn't work. I was determined for some reason to exercise. I really wanted to get on the elliptical however it was down. I almost didn't get on the treadmill at all. Then I did. I wanted to do 45 minutes. As I was on there working and walking and jogging and even doing some periodic sprints, it came to mind, ahhh that's good enough. Then for some reason it hit me like a bolt of lightning right smack dab where I live . . ." I never ever have to stop short of my goal ever again." I can do it and I will do it. Exactly what Frank told me was a life pattern. "Good has always been good enough—just getting by is acceptable." Not anymore. Something sparked, something ignited actually. It doesn't matter if my good is better than what*

some or even most others consider great. My good has to be good for me. I never again will judge my performance on the best or even the worst of someone else's efforts. I will only judge me on my best efforts. The treadmill died at 42 minutes. That little voice inside said, "ahhhh that's good enough" . . . come on you did 42 minutes!" Then I had to reboot it, start over and finish my last 3 minutes. Something has happened and I can't really explain it. I will think about it, meditate about it and write more about it.

*I really believe—**I will never stop short of a goal again***

Dan was searching for more meaning in his life when we first met. In this e-mail you can see what happened when he learned to create a gap between stimulus and response. He was able to recognize that the elevator effect was about to take hold in the exercise room of the hotel. He consciously created a gap and in that gap was able to shift his focus to a goal, which in turn helped him achieve a life overflowing with potential and joy. In this chapter I discuss what I believe is the foundation for a meaningful life, which is *love-based life-controlling patterns.*

For centuries, philosophers have been asking what appears to be an important question: "What is the meaning of life?" And for centuries abstract responses that never really answer the question have been given. I think I know why.

They have been asking the wrong question.

I believe a better question seekers of a meaningful life could ask is, "How do I create a meaningful life?" This starts with the premise that the Divine bestowed on you specialness that only you possess. Your job is to identify your life's mission and the talents you have to support it and then use those talents to live a meaningful life.

Creative seekers are not victims.

Creative seekers know the answers are within, and when you ask the right kind of questions, the answers will appear. Having a meaningful life doesn't mean that you have discovered a cure for cancer. A meaningful life is one where you use your talents to their fullest, whatever your talents are. For some, using their talents will lead to a Nobel Prize, while for others it will mean that they use their talents to nurture and offer a helping hand to those in the community that need it.

My treadmill-using client Dan, who will never stop short of his goal again, is a creative seeker, and he is finding his answers within himself. He is creating life-controlling patterns that are based in love and support who he truly is. He has learned to put a gap between stimulus and response. Love-based life-controlling patterns are now filling the gap and determining his response. He is on his way to creating and living a meaningful life.

The Law of Soul Alignment

A number of years ago, I realized that there was a universal law that had never been clearly articulated. My clients were telling me in their unique ways that their daily lives were not in alignment with their talents. Few if any had a well-thought-out mission statement for their lives. Your soul aches when misalignment occurs between how you are living and what the Divine Intention is for your life.

I created the Law of Soul Alignment as a way to describe what must happen if we are going to experience joy and abundance on a regular basis. *The Law of Soul Alignment says that joy and abundance will occur in your life when there is alignment between what you are being day in and day out with what you were sent here to be.*

To fully appreciate The Law of Alignment, I need to explain several of the words in it. When I speak of *joy,* I am talking about that feeling you have deep inside when you know you are fully connected to your Self, others, and the Divine. Joy is an inside job and is the result of perfect alignment. For me, joy is different than being happy. Being happy for most people is the result of an external occurrence. Happiness comes when someone gives you something or does something nice for you. Happiness is a nice feeling, but it is much less powerful than joy. I believe the Divine intended for us to be joyful and to use our joy to influence the world around us. *Joy is not another word for putting on rose-colored glasses and making believe. Joy is a powerful energy that arises when you are being you.*

To some, *abundance* relates only to money, while to others it has a much broader definition. My use here is in the broader terms. Abundance is whatever you define it to be. I encourage you to write down what abundance means to you. If you haven't defined it, how will you know when you have achieved it? If you haven't defined it, how will you know you are in alignment?

Alignment is another word that I believe requires understanding beyond its definition. There are several things that one must do to be in alignment. First off, being aligned with who you were sent here to be requires that you are very clear about the mission for your life. Your mission must be written. Here's my mission statement: *My mission in life is to experience the joy of living on purpose and sharing what I learn with other seekers.*

Not only do you need to write it, you must also live it. When you are being the real you, connections with others and the Divine flourish. If you still find yourself saying, "I don't know what I want to be when I grow up," you haven't reached alignment. But if you can honestly say, "I love my life," that is a strong indicator that you have embraced The Law of Soul Alignment

When you make The Law of Soul Alignment operational in your life, your soul will stop aching.

I recently met with a person who had a clear soul alignment problem, and his soul and body were literally aching. Larry is a talented artist who has several ways in which he expresses his creativity. One is photography and the other is sculpting in stone. Unfortunately, neither of these outlets was being utilized. He earned a living doing photography, but not the creative type he loved to do. His business was primarily taking photographs of products his clients market. Nothing creative, just take the shot and make the product look good. He hadn't touched his sculpting tools in five years. There was no alignment between what he was being and what he was sent here to be. The photography was close, but it wasn't fully aligned. By the way, Larry was having trouble sleeping through the night. It is difficult to sleep when day after day you know you have a superior talent and it is not being used. Larry is a very high-energy person who had learned to keep the lid on his creative side.

In order for Larry to sleep better and feel more joy, he needed alignment between what he was being day in and day out with what he was sent here to be. The energy of a fulfilled soul cannot flow when the valve of alignment is

shut off. Create alignment and the valve opens, allowing a magnificent flow of energy to and through you. You will feel peacefully supercharged when your soul is aligned with Divine Intent.

Since we began our work together, Larry has aligned his life to what the Divine intended for him. He is now more creative with his photography and is bringing peacefully supercharged energy to almost everything he does.

When you are out of alignment, you rely on adrenaline and anxiety to keep you going. The combination of adrenaline and anxiety is a one-way ticket to poor health, not to mention a sad heart and an empty soul.

As my clients master the art of being themselves and create alignment, they are routinely delighted with how their lives change. For example:

- One client finally addressed serious problems that existed in her relationship. Because she was finally being *herself,* the conversation with her spouse that she had avoided for years was easier and more positive than she could possibly have imagined.
- A talented singer is now focusing on building the singing career he wants and deserves.
- A gentleman stuck in the wrong job is now writing the book that will lead to the speaking career he wants.
- On the West coast, a dentist now finds it easier to attract the type of patients he desires.
- A nurse who was widowed felt she would never find another partner. She was also working nights and didn't like it. At this point she is engaged, working days, and about to launch another career.

I know that it is possible to experience the alignment that results in joy filling your life. I intend to teach you how to create that alignment. The path to alignment is simple; however, it is not easy.

The secret to leading a meaningful life is to develop life-controlling patterns that are in alignment with your mission and your talents. Alignment won't occur until you have shifted from a life dominated by fear and the life-controlling patterns it generates to one powered by life-controlling patterns that are based on love.

Fear-based life-controlling patterns create deficiency and suffering in our lives. They are at the core of why we take actions to control people, places, and things. The end result of a life dominated these patterns will be less than meaningful. For many people it takes decades to realize that if they continue on their current paths they will die, as Oliver Wendell Holmes said, "with the music still in you." When the Law of Soul Alignment is operating for you, at the end of your time, you will be sliding in broadside shouting, "Wow, what a ride!"

The difference between life-controlling patterns based on fear and those based on love is much more than just substituting one word for another. The energy at which love-based patterns operate is geometrically higher than that of fear-based patterns. The emotion of love, when it directs the majority of our life-controlling patterns, leads to a meaningful life and tends to be a complete connection with your Self, others, and the Divine.

Love-based life-controlling patterns have the same components as fear-based ones—but with vastly different result. **Remember, emotion is the determining factor in life-controlling patterns!** In love-based life-controlling patterns, the emotion that is felt is love. In fear-based life-controlling patterns, the emotion is fear. The acronym for fear is False Expectations Appearing Real, which I believe captures the essence of these life patterns. I decided I needed the same type of essence-capturing acronym for love. The result is:

Living
On
Vibrant
Energy

Love-based life patterns give you a sense that you are living on vibrant energy that consistently flows to and through you. You become peacefully supercharged when they direct your behavior.

Whatever we plant in our subconscious mind and nourish with repetition and emotion will one day become a reality.—Earl Nightingale

The actions that are taken in love-based life-controlling patterns are creative, and as a result you will become aligned with who you really are.

When you are living with love-based life patterns, there is a huge gap between stimulus and response that you can fill with a wide assortment of possibilities, regardless of the situation you are facing. There is little worry about producing a safe result because you realize that the white light of the Divine always protects you. This doesn't mean you live recklessly. It just means that you are not afraid to do things that are in alignment with your unique set of talents. It means that when the elevator door of opportunity opens, you are prepared to go for it. You know that by exploring your talents, you are fulfilling the Divine's mission for you. And as you live in alignment, you have and create more energy. Instead of life being a struggle, it is effortless. That doesn't mean you don't have problems; it means that the problems don't cause things to come to a halt. You find a way forward.

Taking creative actions means that you give up trying to control everyone. It means that you see the bright light of potential and capability in others and yourself. It means that you listen differently. You choose to listen for the ideas and potential in what others are saying. You choose not to look for what is wrong or to find fault in others ideas. Taking creative actions that are the outcome of love-based life-controlling patterns means that you recognize that no one knows all of the answers and that each of us has a vision of a part of the truth.

Our desire in love-based life patterns is that our actions result in everyone being able to operate for the highest possible good. When I say everyone, I mean everyone including ourselves. When fear-based life patterns are operating, people often take actions that are good for everyone with no thought of their own well-being. If you are living a life of self-sacrifice, always putting others first, never worrying about what is good you, you end up being exhausted. If you are not taking care of yourself, you are limiting the real energy you have to contribute to the rest of the world.

In love-based life patterns, you lose your attachment to the correctness or magnificence of the result. In every result you experience the seed of new learning and the possibility of new input that will lead to enhanced life patterns. Regardless of the result, you are capable of exclaiming, "How fantastic!"

Love-based life-controlling patterns produce openness to Divine wisdom. When you are capable of sorting new input in an open and fearless way, the door to constant new learning and adaptation is consistently before you. What was once a closed-loop system, where the same limited number of actions was repeated over and over again, is now an open system where there are a limitless number of possibilities and actions.

As I've pointed out many times now, we are programmed with fear-based life controlling patterns very early in life. That is the bad news. Most of us are fighting an uphill battle against fears that are programmed into our subconscious. The good news is that love-based life-controlling patterns were also programmed into us early in life, and they are just as powerful. Best of all, you have the ability to can create even more love-based patterns so that you live in alignment.

Let me give you some examples of life-controlling patterns that are based on love.

- My wife's mother was a person who was fully engaged with life and had the ability to make everything a party and a joyous event. As a result, my wife learned to create joy wherever she is.

- Maria learned from her father the importance being logical and focusing on the task at hand. This led to a successful thirty-year career in project management in telecommunications.

- Bob was fortunate to grow up in an environment where committing to tasks that are important in life and sticking with them until they are through was revered. This life pattern that aligns with his talents has enabled him turn a struggling manufacturing firm into one the most profitable and best in its niche. The company achieved 20 percent growth in this down economy.

- In my childhood home everyone was always welcome. My mother offered a helping hand and place to stay for several individuals. She passed along to me a capacity for empathy and compassion, which is of untold importance in my coaching career. It also enabled me to provide a home for my nephew, who was struggling with drugs and alcohol. I was incredibly happy the day I saw him get his diploma.

Love-based patterns are those patterns stored in your subconscious that trigger the emotion of love and are in alignment with Natural Law.

They support your mission in life. They embrace your unique God-given talents and lead to application of your talents. What life-controlling patterns based on love are resident in you?

Fear-based patterns result in "I can't" feelings and statements. Love-based patterns show you that you can. In most if not all of the examples and stories I have shared about clients, you can see the shift from "I can't" to "I can," or from the low energy of fear to the powerful energy of love.

As human beings evolved, the subconscious mind, through its vast power to scan the world around us and take in what is occurring, has become our guardian and protector. It is always on full alert to determine if we are physically and/or emotionally safe. From the time of our ancient ancestors, the subconscious mind has been trained to look for what is wrong. The result is that human beings have become experts at finding fault with our environment and ourselves. Fear is the filter through which we see the world.

In the beginning of this chapter I suggested you underline the words that are important to you. I encourage you to digest the next paragraph.

Successful, joyful people have learned to change what the subconscious is looking for. Joyful people who consistently experience abundance learned to shift the subconscious from scanning for what is wrong with a situation to finding what is possible and how they can use their talents to the fullest in a situation. Every self-insight book you have ever read is about shifting what the subconscious is focused on. Shortly I will give you a very effective and simple exercise to do that. Mastering the art of creating and installing love-based life patterns in the subconscious is the key to leading a meaningful life that is in alignment with what your soul intends for you to be. You must change what your subconscious is looking for to explode the potential you were born with.

Chapter 8

Shift Happens

Pop quiz time. How will you know that the shift has happened in your life? How will you know that you have shifted from a life dominated by fear to one where you are living on vibrant energy and you are experiencing a very meaningful life?

Simple—you will recognize that a shift happened when you experience the ten clues that you now have Positive Energy Syndrome (PES). Positive Energy Syndrome is present in you when key life-controlling patterns are love-based and in alignment with your talents and your mission in life. It is impossible to have a meaningful life without having Positive Energy Syndrome.

Top Ten (Plus One) Clues You Have Positive Energy Syndrome

1. You frequently find yourself saying, "How fantastic!"
2. You love what you do.
3. You have created rituals that help you maintain your faith.
4. You easily see how Negative Energy Syndrome operates in others, and you love them anyway.
5. Feedback is something you cherish and never take personally.
6. Because you easily put a gap between stimulus and response, you always find a way.
7. Your body gets the fuel it needs every day.
8. You have a mission statement that you can recite easily, and a twelve-year-old could understand it.

9. You acknowledge and monitor your emotions.
10. Your capacity to love and be loved is enormous.
11. It's okay if you let others take care of themselves.

The shift to the Positive Energy Syndrome won't happen unless you apply the four Cs of Big Change: Courage, Commitment, Compassion, and Clarity. If you are like me, when you look at the list of clues, you feel a sense of encouragement and a knowledge that the shift will be worth it.

The results of Positive Energy Syndrome are a struggle-free life; continual high levels of connection with Self, others, and the Divine; ease of manifesting what you want; an open communications flow (even with difficult people); and an enhanced ability to solve life's most difficult challenges. You become a marvelous communicator, spreading joy wherever you go, and your body is incredibly healthy.

Several years ago I was coaching a fifty-plus year old woman who had the fear-based life pattern that she was not smart enough to be promoted to a manager's position. As a result she viewed her career opportunities and her income as limited. She was resigned to staying in her current position, never becoming a manager, and renting a room in her home to generate the money to pay the mortgage. Oh, did I mention that she was commuting sixty minutes each way to work and she hated it? My client perceived herself as a very happy person in spite of the challenges she was facing. She was using humor to hide her sadness about not getting what she wanted from life. Within three months of our working together, she created a love-based life pattern in which she saw herself as an effective manager making the money she wanted. She became a very joyful person. The result was she got a promotion, was able to work from an office that was closer to home, and she didn't have to rent out the room.

When love-based life-controlling patterns are at the core of your life, you will become peacefully supercharged. When you are peacefully supercharged, there is a sense of excitement and urgency about you. It is driven by knowing that you are living with purpose. It is sustained by the endorphins that are created in your body as the result of the way in which you are living. This is different from being an adrenaline addict. High amounts of adrenaline are produced when fear is present inside of you. Adrenaline leads to a frenetic pace that is only sustainable for short periods of time. A peacefully supercharged life can be sustained indefinitely because its primary source of energy, your connection to the Divine, is inexhaustible.

You will know the Positive Energy Syndrome is at work when you consistently know that:

- You can transform any situation.
- You can always see what there is to learn in every interaction.
- You can always find a way.
- You can turn lemons into lemonade.
- You can create wonderful connections with others, anywhere, anytime.
- You can consistently create a gap between stimulus and response.
- You can share your opinion and have it heard and appreciated.
- You can be a powerful and effective leader.
- You can ___(fill in the blank).

What if 50 percent of the population had Positive Energy Syndrome? What would the world be like? What would your life be like if everyone in your family had Positive Energy Syndrome? What would your life be like if you could consciously shift to a love-based life-controlling pattern any time you wanted? What if your capacity to experience heaven is linked to your ability to create the Positive Energy Syndrome in your life?

Just because you have Positive Energy Syndrome doesn't mean you won't have problems and struggles in your life. You will continue to have problems. The difference is that now you won't be stuck trying the same old solutions over and over again. When you have PES, you are no longer a victim. You know that you can find a solution to the problems you encounter in your life. Tapping into the universal wisdom will become something you enjoy.

Joy is something that most of us have to learn how to feel on a regular basis. Being consistently joyful is not what we were taught. Instead we were taught to do what we need to do to fit in—i.e., don't rock the boat. Even though fear-based life-controlling patterns operate on a subconscious level, their constant presence precludes you from regularly feeling joy.

I am coaching a wonderful, spiritual woman who loved to dream as a child. She could see creative opportunities all around her. However, when her father thought that she was "day-dreaming," he would criticize her. He told her to take off the rose-colored glasses and be practical. At the age of sixty-three, she is learning to dream again and to not always be practical. She has learned to feel joy on a consistent basis.

By the time I have explained life-controlling patterns and the power that exists in the love-based ones, my clients have already asked several times, "How do you do it?" They have already gone the positive thinking route and come up short on their Big Change. They want something that is simple to remember, easy to do, and proven to be effective.

When I give them the answer, they don't believe me. But then they try it and realize it works!

I would like to share with you the secret to creating the love-based energy that makes the shift happen and results in a meaningful life.

Chapter 9

The Master Key—The Smile Exercise

The way to overcome negative thoughts and destructive emotions is to develop opposing, positive emotions that are stronger and more powerful.—Dalai Lama

Helen had been a reluctant participant in the teleclass. Her friend, who had experienced wonderful success with the class, had convinced her to take it. In the first two classes Helen didn't say much, and when she did it was to question the validity of what I was presenting. As I began to explain the secret to creating powerful love-based life-controlling patterns that support your mission and talents, Helen interrupted and said, "It can't be that simple!" I asked her to just try my process for the next two weeks. Helen reluctantly agreed. At the start of the next teleclass, she quietly admitted, "Yes, it is that simple to create a new way of life."

Stop right now!

Put a gap between stimulus and response and ask yourself if you are ready to create your own life patterns that are joy-producing and fulfilling.

You could choose to be satisfied with the life patterns your parents and others gave you. That will most likely result in continual stress because you know something is missing in your life.
Which do you want?

Either choice is okay; just make a conscious choice. If you want change, dive into the next few pages and devour the information. If you are not ready to make the Big Change yet, casually read this chapter knowing that you will learn some information that could be a conversation starter at a party.

By now you are probably saying to yourself, Frank, let's get on with this. How do you make the shift from a limiting, fear-based life to an ever expanding, love-based life?

As I noted before, the positive-thinking gurus suggest that if you think a thought a thousand times, it will come true. They barely mention the power of emotion in making changes in your life. The universally accepted behavioral model I presented on life-controlling patterns clearly shows the power of emotion in our lives. To recap, the model flows like this:

- Input
- Thought
  - Conscious
  - Subconscious
- Emotion
- Action
- Result

Notice that action follows the emotion. Thoughts do not produce action, emotion leads to action. If you are wondering why you haven't had the results you want from positive thinking, you now have the answer. Positive thoughts must be combined with the powerful emotion of love.

Here is the real secret: Until you change your emotion, you won't change your life pattern. When you change the emotion, you will start the action that you need to live a love-based life pattern. You start the change by taking control of the emotion, not the thought.

In the life pattern model, an emotion is generated as soon as the input is recognized in the subconscious. Going back to the fear-based life pattern I mentioned earlier about money, no matter how often you think "I am a millionaire," fear will occur inside of you until you learn to associate money with the emotion of love.

You must learn to generate the emotion of love when you are making the shift from a fear-based life to a love-propelled life. Permanent powerful change in your life is driven by the emotion of love or, if you prefer, joy. Thoughts alone won't do it. Will power, research has shown, is a limited resource. Will power is driven by your conscious mind. When the conscious mind gets tired, the ever vigilant subconscious mind takes over making the change. The subconscious relies on emotion attached to the thought pattern to determine if you are safe. The learned emotion that goes with the thought will always dominate. That is why changes you have attempted to think your way through in the past haven't worked. The conscious mind gets tired, the subconscious takes over, and the old fears kick in. For example, let's say you have decided to speak up and let others know what you are thinking. No longer is your old fear of being criticized going to dominate your life. During the first week, it works well for you. Then in week two you are at a meeting and suddenly your manager asks your opinion. The conscious mind lets its guard down, the old fear-based life pattern stored in the subconscious pops up, and you are unable to articulate your real ideas on what should be done.

Several years ago I was coaching a man who owned three health food stores. His goal was to expand his business and earn over $1 million per year. During our second coaching call, while we were discussing life controlling patterns, he said, "Frank, I have started numerous self-improvement programs, and after about six weeks I lose interest and give up. I have been working on changing my thoughts for a long time. Why is that happening?" What was happening was that his conscious mind/will power gave out and his subconscious took over. He had a fear-based life pattern that people with money were bad. He came from a coal mining town and the rich folks, it was said, got their money illegally or off the backs of the miners. No matter how much his conscious mind wanted to identify with being rich, his subconscious mind identified money with the fear of being perceived as a bad person. It wasn't until he changed the emotion regarding rich people that he was able to make the change. When his mother visited him after he built his dream home, her first question to him as she walked in the front door was, "Son, where did you get the money to build this home? Are you up to no good?"

Learning to shift from fear to love and be able to consistently experience life-controlling patterns that are joy-driven is simple.

You can switch your emotion very quickly by doing an easy yet powerful exercise. Simply put a small smile on your face and hold it for ten seconds. You will be amazed what this will do for how you feel. Try it right now. Smile for ten seconds. While you are smiling, notice what is happening inside of you. How did it feel? Whenever I do this exercise in seminars, participants tell me they feel lighter, or they feel calmer, or they want to start to laugh. Whatever the outcome, the change is almost instantaneous for most people.

Increasing the consistency with which you feel love/high energy will increase your ability to manifest what you want in your life.

When you smile, you automatically change your physiology. Smiling gives you enhanced access to the power of your brain to create. It is a scientific fact that two things can't occupy the same space at the same time. When you have a smile on your face, the debilitating force of fear is diminished.

Based on what I learned about smiling and knowing that you must change your emotion to change your life pattern, I created what I call the smile exercise. The goal of the smile exercise is to enable you to create love-based life patterns that are in alignment with what you were sent here to be.

The smile exercise automatically increases the gap between stimulus and response. It is in the gap where all of the possibilities for your life exist. The smile exercise opens up your creativity, enabling you to experience a limitless flow of energy from the Divine.

The smile exercise is a simple process that consists of:

1. Getting a smile on your face
2. Consciously feeling the energy flowing through you that is created by your smile.
3. Visualizing yourself acting in alignment with the positive change you want to make while you continue to feel the energy of your smile.
4. Saying a declaration that describes how you want to be.

Let me give you an example of how this works. I had a client, whom I shall refer to as Susan, who had the fear-based life-controlling pattern that her opinion was not valued and should seldom be expressed. The pattern was the result of receiving input at a very young age that if and when Susan expressed her opinion, she would be criticized. What she learned was to keep her mouth shut and she wouldn't be criticized. When I started coaching with Susan, she was in her forties and experiencing problems on her job and in her marriage because she was unable to share her ideas. The fear-based life pattern caused her to think that she was defective. She wasn't. She was just doing what she had learned as a youngster. Susan wanted to be able to speak her mind and influence what was happening in her life.

Once we knew what the fear was, we created a smile exercise for her. I start the creation of the smile exercise by developing a declaration that captures the love-based action that will generate the desired result. The desired result was that she could express her opinion and influence what happened in her life. The declaration we used was, "I easily share my opinions and ideas with others."

I coached Susan to get the smile on her face, feel the energy flowing, visualize herself sharing her ideas with her husband and then declaring out loud, " I easily share my opinions and ideas with others."

This smile exercise worked wonders for Susan. She made adjustments in her job so that it became more enjoyable, and she is creating the relationship she wants with her husband. As an added benefit, her adult daughters are now seeing and learning how to create more of what they want in their lives.

Feeling joy and creating the life we desire is not something we are accustomed to doing. To create the life you want that matches your potential, you must create new neural pathways that lead to the feeling of love. Love and joy are found by filling the gap between stimulus and response with love-based life patterns.

Your life patterns have been operating for decades. The smile exercise is the master key to changing your deeply entrenched life patterns.

Hal participated in several of my teleclasses. He never said much. He was a man who believed in action, not words. However, Hal surprised me in the next-to-the-last class of the second series in which he participated. We were discussing the success people had in their lives since our last teleclass. Hal spoke up, saying, "Frank, I was little skeptical about your smile exercise, but I did it anyway. I have never told anyone what I am about to say, but I want you to know how these classes have affected me. All of my life, the first thing I think about in the morning is committing suicide. I never would attempt it, but I have the thought. I didn't like having that thought, but I could never stop it. Since I started doing the smile exercise, I have not had that thought in the morning. My life is moving in the right direction."

The smile exercise is simple and powerful!

The following are the steps for using the smile exercise effectively:

Steps for Creating Love-based Life-Controlling Patterns

Step # 1: Become aware of the fear-based life pattern that is operating in your subconscious. Notice when you hesitate, procrastinate, make excuses, or just don't do things that tap into your talents and potential. For example, you might notice that you just can't seem to make it to the next income level you would like to achieve.

Step #2: Identify the fear-based life patterns you want to change. Describe what the fear is. For example: I don't believe that someone like me deserves to make a lot of money.

Step # 3: Create a declaration for the love-based life pattern.

Focus on describing the essence of the emotion and action you want to experience in your new life pattern. For example: I deserve money and abundance, and it flows easily to me. A declaration is not saying something is true, it's stating that we have an intention of doing or being something. This is a position the little voice inside of each of us can buy because we are not stating it is true right now. It is an intention for the future. A declaration, by definition, is also official. It is a formal statement of energy into the Universe and throughout your body. Another word from the definition is important—action. You must take the actions necessary to make your intention a reality.

So what's the point here? Start making *declarations* for what you truly want, and then take the necessary *action*. Then you will see how the Law of Attraction works when you apply both declaration and action!

Step #4: Do the smile exercise and feel the energy flowing through you.

- Get a slight smile on your face.
- Feel the energy flowing through your body.
- In your mind's eye, see yourself doing the action in your declaration.
- Now say the declaration.

Step #5: Repeat the smile exercise thirty times a day for thirty days.

The objective is to create a new neural pathway that is automatically recognized in your subconscious. Remember you have to overcome decades of living a fear-based life pattern. You can do the thirty repetitions all at once, or ten in the morning, ten at lunch, and ten in the evening, or any other combination you choose. Just do thirty per day. At the most this will take two and a half minutes of your time. Is the life of your dreams worth two and a half minutes a day?

Step #6: Have courage and continue the process even when you feel like giving up.

Change of the magnitude we are talking about does not come easily.

Courage is mandatory. The ego will do whatever is necessary to defend what it perceives as real. As you make the shift to a life where love and joy are predominate, the ego will see its job as Engaging God's Opportunities. Making the change is worth it, but it takes lots of hard work and courage to believe in yourself and your potential.

Step #7: Begin taking actions that are consistent with your claration. For example, if your declaration is similar to Susan's, begin by stating your opinion in easy and safe situations. For example, if your spouse asks you, "Where would you like to go for dinner?" Instead of saying, "I don't care," express your preference. "I want to go to the Italian restaurant on Main Street." Begin taking simple actions that start to move you in the direction you want to go.

Step # 8: Keep a record of your declarations and the successes as you make the changes you desire.

Melody embraced the smile exercise as I explained it to her in one of our coaching sessions. Just before going to sleep, she would say her declaration out loud, "I easily connect with other people." During a coaching call several months into our coaching process, she told me that one night the previous week she had skipped doing the smile exercise. She was about to drift off to sleep when her husband reminded her that she hadn't done it. He also added that she had been a much happier person since doing it, and he loved seeing her that way.

A benchmark of emotional management and responsibility is the realization that our past can no longer be blamed for our actions in the present.—Doc Childre and Howard Martin, *The HeartMath Solution*

Some people have a difficult time developing the declaration for the smile exercise. Here are few that I have created:

- Joy and abundance flow easily to me.
- I easily manage money.
- I love myself.
- I am an effective and efficient manager.

- I easily and powerfully share my ideas with others.
- I am an effective and entertaining speaker.
- I easily get the love I want and deserve.
- I easily connect with other people.
- I easily live a life of grace and ease.
- I easily ask others for help.

The list of declarations suggests that there are many love-based life patterns that you can create. By now you have probably identified several fear-based life-controlling patterns that you want to change. Clients frequently ask me, "How many life patterns and smile exercises can I work on at the same time?" My recommendation is that you work on one at a time as you are getting started. At least for the first thirty days, one is enough. Most of my clients have two to three major fear-based life patterns that limit the joy in their lives. When you study and apply this process for a while, you will find that there are many more life-controlling patterns hidden from view that gradually reveal themselves as you achieve higher and higher levels of your potential. In a joy-filled life, learning never stops.

Here are a few examples of the impact that the smile exercise has had on people's lives.

Julie had been a client for several months and the smile exercise was really elevating her joy of life. She was feeling very good about her life and her business as she did her smile exercises while stopped at a traffic light on the way to a meeting. She didn't know until later that Sara, a friend of hers, was in the car right behind and she could see Julie smiling in the rear view mirror. Also unbeknownst to Julie, Sara's day was off to a horrible start. A few days later Julie ran into Sara, who told Julie she could see her smiling when they were at the stoplight. She related how miserable she had been feeling when she pulled up behind Julie. As a result of seeing Julie's great smile and sensing the energy, her mood lightened and the rest of her day was marvelous. Don't underestimate the power of your smile, even reflected in the rear view mirror.

In a blog I posted recently, I talked about the power of the smile. A reader posted this comment:

> *As I was staring off into space during my morning commute, I noticed the woman across from me scrolling through*

her messages on her phone, and then after reading something, she had a huge smile on her face. Even though I didn't know her or what she was reading, her smile was contagious! Merely observing another's smile seems to have a positive impact on one's mood.

Here is another. Pat was a participant in my Change Your Energy—Change Your Life series of teleclasses. She was an eager participant who really wanted to take her life and her business to the next level. Pat and her husband were moving from the Midwest to the West coast. Their plan was to drive west, spend a few weeks looking for a new place, hopefully find one, buy it, and then make the move. Pat was fearful that they wouldn't find a place that they liked and could afford. During the drive, Pat continuously did the smile exercise, using the declaration that she would easily find the perfect home. Within several days of arriving in their new hometown, they found the perfect home!

John is a client who had the fear that he was not capable of creating and sustaining success in any area of his life, from his tennis game to his business to his home. When he perceived that something was going wrong, he would have a panic attack. His panic attacks were always the impetus for his self-fulfilling prophecy of being unable to sustain success. Over time, as he did the smile exercise, declaring that he was a capable and successful person, his panic attacks diminished and he has sustained over several years now a level of success that he once told me he couldn't achieve.

As you can see, understanding life patterns and doing the smile exercise has helped many different types of people in many different ways. I have not had clients use the smile exercise to lose weight, but one of the side effects of eliminating fear for many clients has been better managing their weight. If you want to use it for losing weight, I suggest that your declaration be "I easily achieve my perfect body weight!"

Creating loving yet structured relationships with children in today's world can be challenging, especially if you have life patterns about raising children that are heavy on the "do as I say" model. Or it could be that fears and stresses in other areas of your life result in interactions with your children that don't match how you want to be with them. In those instances, I suggest that you use the declaration "I easily create loving and effective relationships with my children." Combine this with actions that you know will result in loving interactions, such as playing a game or going for a walk.

The applications of this process are limitless.

Remember the Law of Soul Alignment—joy and abundance will occur in your life whey there is alignment between what you are being day in and day out with what you were sent here to be. The secret to creating a life that is in alignment is to implant in your subconscious love-based life patterns that are in alignment with who you really are.

Learning and doing the smile exercise opens the door to being who you were sent here to be. The smile exercise, done thirty times a day for thirty days and combined with actions, will cement your soul-aligned, love-based life-controlling patterns firmly in place.

Caution! The changes you are seeking happen over a period of time and may be in forms you don't recognize. There is a power in the smile exercise that sneaks up on people. In coaching sessions I always discuss with clients their successes and victories since our last call. Not long ago I was talking to a couple that I had been working with for two months. One of their successes since our last call was that they had a great meeting with three new potential clients for their business. They acknowledged that this happened because they were more relaxed. However, they did not connect their relaxation with the smile exercise. The smile exercise was having a transformative effect on them. Even the tone of their voices was different. Laughter was present throughout our discussion, where in prior calls there had been little or no laughter. As you do the smile exercise, please pay attention to the small things that are changing in your life. Give yourself and the smile exercise credit for the successes you achieve. Don't overlook them.

I have noticed that there is a tendency to think that major events that happen to us are what change our lives. That is not true. Earlier I discussed how joy and abundance are the result of doing things in a certain way. I wrote, "I can form things with my emotions, and by impressing my emotions upon formless substance, I can cause the thing I feel to be created." Building on that concept, I created The Law of Repetition. It says, *your life is the result of the input, thoughts, emotions and actions you repeat over and over and over again. Your life is not the result of one event. Change what you repeat and you will change your life. Nothing is forever, things change. Life is a never-ending series of temporary events.*

As you repeat the smile exercise over and over again, notice how events in your life change. Notice how you are accomplishing things you thought you would never do. Notice how little miracles in your life continue to occur until you wake up one morning and realize your life is what you wanted.

Chapter 10

For the Doubters

In case you still doubt the power of the smile exercise, I am including some research on the effects of smiling over and above its effect on the creation of love-based life-controlling patterns.

Here is a portion of what I found.

In the *Journal of Personality and Social Psychology,* C. L. Kleinke, T. R. Peterson, and T. R. Rutledge reported in a 1998 article titled "Effect of Self-Generated Facial Expressions" that:

- People who smile frequently are perceived as being more confident and successful.
- Most people are more inclined to start a conversation with a stranger when the stranger is smiling.
- People who smile a lot have a better chance of being promoted.
- Your smile is so powerful that it will have a positive impact on phone conversations.
- Research shows that happiness is the result of smiling, contrary to what most people think.

Here is a list of various research projects and what they indicated that smiling could do.

- Increased cognitive flexibility (Ashby, et al. 1999)
- Improved memory (Isen, et al. 1978)
- Improved decision making (Carnevale & Isen 1986)

- Increased creativity and innovative problem solving (Isen, et al. 1987)
- Improved job performance & achievement (Wright & Staw 1994)
- Improved clinical problem solving (Estrada, et al.1997)
- Increased longevity (Danner, et al. 2001)
- Reduced morbidity (Goldman, et al 1996; Russek & Schwartz 1997)

One of my favorite reports on the power of a smile came from an article I found on the web at www.SixWise.com. The title of the article is "Smile! The Remarkable Personal Benefits of Smiling." In the article it said:

Smiling Feels Like Eating 2,000 Chocolate Bars

The British Dental Health Foundation reports that a smile produces the same level of stimulation as eating 2,000 chocolate bars. A healthy smile can improve your confidence, help you make friends, and help you to succeed in your career.

If you enjoy chocolate as much as I do, you will understand the unbelievable impact smiling has on me if it is the equivalent of two thousand chocolate bars.

Mark Stibich, PhD, created the Top 10 Reasons to Smile, which I found at About.com (http://longevity.about.com/od/lifelongbeauty/tp/smiling.htm, updated February 4, 2010). His reasons included that

- smiling makes us more attractive,
- smiling elevates your mood,
- smiling relives stress,
- smiling releases endorphins, and
- smiling makes it easier for you to stay positive.

All of these research projects help to verify the law of physics that tells us that two things cannot occupy the same place at the same time. Therefore if you are smiling, then fear cannot be present at the same time.

Chapter 11

Finding True North

The apprehension is always high as we start the third session of the Change Your Energy—Change Your Life teleclass. Between the second and third class the assignment is to write the mission statement for your life. I define mission statement as a short, simple sentence that articulates the core reason for your being in this world. For example, the mission statement for my life is *to experience the power of living on purpose and sharing what I learn with other seekers.*

One of the major roadblocks people hit when writing mission statements is that they feel that they must create the perfect mission statement. They feel if they don't get it right, they will be stuck with an incorrect, self-defeating mission statement for the rest of their lives and their lives will be incomplete. At the end of class two, when I give the assignment on mission statements, I inform them that I will ask each of them to say their mission statement out loud to the class. I also let them know that I will probably be doing some coaching to help them to fine tune what they have written. As we start the mission statement class, I can tell, even though we are on the phone, that everyone has their heads down, hoping that I will not call on them first.

Rachel, who loves life and is a hard-charging person who has never met an obstacle she couldn't overcome, didn't have her head down when I asked who would like to go first on this Wednesday evening class. She volunteered right away and guardedly said her mission statement. My sense was that she was very close to having a well-crafted mission. Like most of my clients, she had the intent correct but was using too many words. I gave her some coaching on how to improve it, and she revised it to say, "My mission is to joyfully use my wisdom to connect others to their greatness." As Rachel repeated the short, simple sentence, her tears began to flow. She said, "Frank, this feels so right and so good that I can't help crying." Rachel had found her True North. It took her four decades to find out why she was on earth. Now there was a clear and positive direction to her life that was driven by the energy of love. She had the courage to write it down and then say it out loud.

Everyone I have coached or taught in a teleclass agrees that they would like to have a clear mission for their lives. It is just that fear gets in the way and procrastination takes over. There is always an excuse for not taking the time to write a mission statement. The excuses include:

- A mission statement is hard work, and what if I get it wrong—I will be stuck with it for the rest of my life.
- I have done it before, and it never really helped. The statement was long, and I can't even remember what was in it. I was forced to do it in a workshop I attended.
- If I have an accurate and effective mission statement, then I will no longer be able to say, "I don't know what I want to be when I grow up." Although flimsy, my excuse for not using my talents will disappear.
- It will provide an opportunity for friends and family to criticize what I write. They don't believe in the real me anyway.

Which one of these have you used, or do you have a different one?

If your desire is to live a meaningful life and experience the Law of Alignment while making the Law of Attraction work for you, then you need to break through all of your fears about mission statements. In my own life and in the lives of the hundreds of people I have helped write mission statements, nothing has led to a greater sense of peace and direction than completing a well-crafted mission statement.

I have learned that writing a mission statement is easier after my clients have gained insights about themselves through exploring life-controlling patterns. Your mission statement is your guide, your True North, for love-based life-controlling patterns that create alignment between what you are being every day and what you were sent here to be.

Your mission statement puts into writing what the Divine intended you to be. Without one your life is like a rudderless ship in a storm—you will be bounced around and feel totally out of control. With a mission statement for a guide, you will find that the four Cs of Big Change (courage, commitment, compassion, and clarity) are easier to master. It is impossible to have clarity about the direction for your life without a mission statement.

When you are ready to write the mission statement for your life, use the following process:

Step 1. Set aside sixty to ninety minutes to be alone. I know that may be difficult for many people to do. The demands on our time seem to increase on a daily basis. However, the investment of the time to write and then use a mission statement as your guide is one that will pay off in more ways than I can articulate.

Step 2. Pick a place in which you feel peaceful and creative. Once you are alone and ready to begin the process, start by getting relaxed. Use your favorite relaxation technique—mediation, deep breathing, listening to music—whatever works best for you.

Step 3. I recommend that you use a structured process for creating your mission statement. Coming up with your mission from scratch without some form of guidance is difficult. With my clients I use the process Laurie Beth Jones outlined in her book *The Path*. Her mission-writing process begins by selecting three action verbs that describe who you are at your core. You will find a comprehensive list of action verbs in her book. The second step is write out what it is you want to stand for—what is your core value? Finally, identify who it is you are here to help. The three verbs, core value, and who your target group is can be combined to create your mission statement.

Before you get to actually composing your mission statement, take out a blank piece of paper and at the top of the page in big bold letters write the word DRAFT. This is to remind yourself that your mission statement doesn't have to be perfect. The mere thought of it having to be perfect can paralyze people, and they can't get started. Give yourself permission to put something on paper as a starting point that you can wordsmith later. Nike says it best, "Just do it!" The DRAFT of your mission statement will be on target when you have a short, easily understood sentence. Short and simple causes many people to struggle. The most effective mission statements can be memorized quickly and easily repeated at any time. If you can't memorize it quickly and say it easily, keep editing it down. Long, wordy mission statements have a way of consuming energy as opposed to creating a sense of energy.

Step 4. Once you have a draft, it is time to test it by saying it out loud. You will know it is right when there is an energy that is ignited inside of you when you speak your mission. It will be an energy that you will easily recognize. The words will almost flow from your mouth. Have someone listen to you say it and ask him if he can hear the joy in your voice as you articulate your mission. When you say it for someone who knows you, his response will be that it sounds like who you are. It will resonate with your soul and those around you

Now you have a wonderful draft. It will change somewhat over the years. However, I don't believe the real core of it will ever change. Words will change, who you want to spend time with as you fulfill your mission might be altered, but the essence of what you were sent here to be will not. I am on version 4.0 of my mission statement and the essence is still the same—sharing what I have learned.

Step 5. Mission statements are meant to be used, not hidden away in drawer. The Law of Attraction is based on being able to consistently generate an energy that matches who you are and what you want to bring into your life. Write your mission on sticky notes and put them all over your home, office, car, etc. I have suggested to numerous clients that they write their mission on a name badge and wear it for a day. This is especially powerful if you are attending a networking meeting. Make it your constant guide in life. It is a great aid in time management. We all have difficulty selecting those things on our to-do lists on which we should focus our efforts. To solve that problem, consult with your North Star and ask yourself, *Is this action bringing me closer to my mission, or is it moving me further away?*

Step 6. Finally, use your mission statement as the declaration in a smile exercise. This will add energy to it and help you to associate your mission statement to the emotion of love. It will overcome the worry about not being able to live your mission in this lifetime.

Congratulations! You now have a very effective mission statement that will automatically link you to the Divine every time you think or say it. That is something I hope you do often.

In case you are wondering what a short, simple, easily understood mission statement sounds like, I have listed several of them below. These are just examples. **Do not just pick one and say that one is me. It is important that you go through the process and really own your mission statement.**

The mission I created for my life is *"My mission is to experience the joy of living on purpose, sharing what I learn with other seekers".*

Here are samples of short, simple mission statements that my clients have developed:

My mission is to:

- Pass the gift of giving love to others.
- Create oneness through love, joy, and peace.
- Inspire people to experience joy.
- Help people find their unique voice.
- Create and connect through healing art.
- Live, love, and connect with fun in relationships.
- Energetically share love with others.
- Cocreate in the present moment.
- Express authentic service that inspires.
- Inspire divine excellence and empower people to become their best self.
- Inspire through integrity and joy.

- Love, serve, and give myself with caring to others.
- Impact women who are socially and economically challenged to significant change.
- Blow the lid off the world by awakening the masses to their creative genius.
- Inspire and teach individuals to make history.
- Encourage others to surrender to the miracles of the universe
- Explore life and connect with people who are seeking.
- Inspire people to live their truth.

Regardless of whose process you use, if your mission doesn't meet these criteria, the statement you develop will have minimal impact on your life. A long, rambling sentence that you can't memorize and doesn't generate energy will quickly fade into the past, and someday you will say, "Why did I waste my time on that? Mission statements don't work." And you will be right. A short action-oriented mission statement that invigorates your soul will have a much different effect. It is the master key to unlocking the answer to the question of what you will be when you grow up.

When these simple criteria are met, you will have in your mission statement the vehicle for really enlarging the gap between stimulus and response. Knowing who you are and what your life is about brings with it the ability to communicate in a more impactful way. In my own life as well as the lives of my clients, I have witnessed that as you learn who you are, you can shut down the small, defensive voice in your head that chatters incessantly while you are talking to others. You will be able to focus all of your attention on the other person. You will be able to recognize when the fear-based life-controlling patterns are operating in others. That will enable you to understand that they are not really attacking you, they are just responding through their fear-based life-controlling pattern. It is amazing what you will notice once you diminish your fears and live your mission.

A meaningful life will not be found in the next job or the next car. The way you get meaning in your life is to devote yourself to helping others and creating something that gives you purpose.—Tuesdays with Morrie by Mitch Albom

Chapter 12

There Is No Silver Bullet

Opportunity is missed by most people because it is dressed in overalls and looks like work.—**Thomas Edison**

Several years ago, Terry, one of my favorite clients, said to me," Frank, I feel so wonderful; this peacefully supercharged feeling is magnificent. But I am worried. I don't want to lose this feeling. I am getting more done, being myself, enjoying life, and being more creative than I have ever been. The smile exercise and my mission statement have worked wonders in my life. How do I keep this going? I am afraid it will disappear, and I will never get it back. Help!"

What Terry wanted was a silver bullet that would ensure everything would be wonderful for the rest of her life. I had to tell her I was fresh out of silver bullets/one-time fixes. There is no one-time injection of anything that will permanently put you in a place of love and joy where alignment flows automatically. I reminded her that life is a never-ending series of temporary events.

The secret to having a joyful and abundant life is not in eliminating or avoiding the rough patches. The secret is in learning to celebrate the temporary events that are joy-filled and being thankful that they occurred while mastering the art of negotiating your way through the difficult experiences, knowing that they are temporary as well. The joys and the fears in life all occur in the never-ending series of gaps between stimulus and response. Being peacefully supercharged on a consistent basis requires that you regularly engage in activities that cause love and joy to flow.

I find it interesting that we so easily forget the things we were doing to open the flow of the energy of Divine Wisdom. I had taught Terry how to create the energy of a meaningful life, and now she wanted something else. She wanted something that was easier, required less effort, and was guaranteed to work for life.

Once you become accustomed to having the Positive Energy Syndrome and being peacefully supercharged, it is very uncomfortable when an old fear-based life-controlling pattern emerges. In order to sustain a meaningful life where the energy of success is consistently present, there are three things that you can do.

1. Consciously engage in those things that enable you to **generate** the energy of love.
2. Once you have generated the energy of love, it is important to **protect** it.
3. It is inevitable that you will encounter the energy of fear, and it will do its best to drag you to your lowest possible level. Therefore, it is important to **cleanse** your energy on a regular basis.

The three-step process then is to GENERATE, PROTECT, and CLEANSE your energy.

Here's how you can do that:

Generate Energy

Just as a great breakfast is an important element in supplying the nutrition you need for a healthy body, the smile exercise is a major part of supplying your body with emotional and spiritual energy you require to make it through the day. When folks first learn the smile exercise, they religiously do it thirty times a day. Doing it that often always produces results for my clients and wonderful stories of how it impacted their lives and the lives of those around them. Invariably after several months of coaching a new challenge will appear in my clients' lives, and they tell me how the new challenge has them befuddled. My first question is, "Are you doing the smile exercise thirty times a day?" Their response is no. They have given up on the thing that made a huge difference in their lives. The smile exercise will work when you work it. First thing in the morning, upon waking, do your smile exercise to create the energy you require to launch your day.

I suggest that you think of your heart as the muscle that produces love and joy. Your heart, like any other muscle, must be exercised if it is to stay fit. The smile exercise will go a long way toward keeping your heart fit. When you do the smile exercise, you are opening your heart and allowing the energy of the Divine to flow to and through you.

Another way of generating energy as you begin your day is to pray or mediate. This doesn't have to take a lot of time, even short prayers begin the flow of the loving energy. The important point is to do something to start the day that puts you into the flow of Divine Energy. Do not start the day worrying about the upcoming events. That is a one-way ticket to a lousy day. For some people, starting the day with exercise and/or being outdoors is their preferred way of launching the energy of success for the day. The list of possibilities goes on and on. Find your way to generate energy and do it every day.

If you have already started making excuses for why you don't have the time to do this, you are not alone. Do you remember the four Cs of Big Change? One on them was courage. To get where you want to be with your life, you need the courage to do the things that are required to make the change. Doing things that will generate energy within you will probably take less than five minutes a day. I encourage you to summon up the courage to do this even when you don't want to.

Consciously do something in the morning that you find generates the energy of the Divine in you.

Protect Your Energy

Most of us have family, friends, or coworkers who are reliable sources of fear and unhappiness. If we let them, they have the capacity to suck the energy right out of us. In order to consistently be peacefully supercharged, it is important to protect the energy that you created as you launched your day.

In order to protect your energy, it will necessary to limit or eliminate the time you spend with the "victims" of the world. Their goal is to get as many people as possible to join them in their fear, anger, and lack of enthusiasm for life. Reject their invitation to participate in whatever manner it takes.

Put a gap between stimulus and response and enable yourself to find ways not to let them impact your world. Limiting or eliminating time with the purveyors of fear in your life is difficult, especially when they are family members or long-time friends. Unfortunately, you don't have a choice if you want a meaningful life in which you consistent experience joy and abundance. After a while of being peacefully supercharged, you will find it very difficult to be in the presence of victims.

Recently one of my clients called me feeling simultaneously happy and sad. He had put a great deal of effort into saving his marriage. Unfortunately his wife continued, as she had done for years, to put her efforts into complaining about their life and everything he did. My client was happy because he finally put a gap between stimulus and response, which enabled him to finally realize how destructive his wife's behavior was. He was working hard at creating the life he wanted, and his spouse was working overtime at pulling him down into her fears. On that day he had decided no more. The price was too high. He asked her to leave. He was sad because he loved her and wanted things to change. However, after years of trying to make it work, he realized that if he was to protect the energy he was creating and build the life he deserved, he could not live with her.

Surrounding yourself with people who are seekers and have the intention of creating the energy of success is a wonderful way to protect your energy. Napoleon Hill, the famous author of *Think and Grow Rich*, referred to these groups as Mastermind. It is a great feeling to know that you can meet with a group that has dedicated itself to helping each person in the group achieve their potential. I belong to one and have facilitated sessions for several other Mastermind groups. I highly recommend that you start one.

If you don't protect the powerful energy of love and joy that you are generating, no one else will.

Cleanse Your Energy

Even if you have been vigilant about protecting your energy, by the end of the day you will still have collected some amount of fear-based energy. It is important to rid yourself of that energy before you go to sleep. By doing this, you will open the way for a better night's rest and a continuation of the flow tomorrow.

Cleansing can be done by simply saying a prayer and focusing on the wonderful things that occurred during the day. Feeling gratitude is a great method for releasing negative energy. Every night before my wife and I go to sleep, we hold hands and pray. That prayer always creates a warm, loving feeling inside of me that enables me to let go of things that are bothersome.

So the three steps to sustaining the energy/love/joy are:

1. Generate
2. Protect
3. Cleanse

On good days, you generate love and joy in the morning, protect your energy through the day, and cleanse your energy at night. On tough days, it may require that you generate, protect, and cleanse every hour. I suggest that you create little sticky notes with these words and place them in many different places as reminders of the process that will enable you create and sustain the energy of success.

There is no one-time fix for making what you have learned in this and other books stick. A meaningful life is the result of creating emotions, thoughts, and actions that match who you really are.

The Law of Soul Alignment, as you may remember, says that **joy and abundance** will occur in your life when there is **alignment** between what you are **being** day in and day out with what you were sent here **to be**. Soul alignment is important because it means that your soul is aligned with the intent the Divine has in mind for it. There is a feeling of peace you have when that alignment occurs. When your soul is out of alignment, there is an ache inside of you that no amount of money, promotions at work, new houses or cars can cure. There is no gap between stimulus and response when you are out of alignment—just rapid reactions that don't produce what you want in life. When you are in alignment, your soul is excited about life because it can't wait to discover what wonderful miracle will happen next. Put simply, you glow and everyone can see it. However, there is a price for that glow. It is to generate, protect, and cleanse at least daily or more often if you need to.

As you learn to sustain the sense of being peacefully supercharged, you will notice that your Gapability is higher. Earlier in the book I asked you to record what your Gapability was and what you wanted it to be. My desire is that by now you will have raised your Gapability score. As you conclude this book, enter your Gapability score as measured today:

Today is _____. I finished the book and my Gapability
is _____.
The most important thing that is different in my life at this
point is _____

Positive emotions have been demonstrated to improve health and increase longevity, increase cognitive flexibility and creativity, facilitate "broadminded coping" and innovative problem solving, and promote helpfulness, generosity, and effective cooperation.—Rollin McCraty, PhD, and Doc Childre, *The Appreciative Heart*

The process of identifying and changing life patterns requires time and effort. Though it may seem daunting, the work is worth it. To determine if you want to put in the effort, please take the following Change Your Life Assessment. Read the eleven statements and place a check next to the ones that are very important to you.

The Change Your Life Assessment

___I want a life that is by and large struggle-free and effortless.

___I want to put all of my talents and potential to full use.

___I want to have meaningful connections with the important people in my life.

___I want to earn the money I am worth.

___I want to powerfully communicate my ideas.

___I want to peacefully drift off to sleep every night.

___I want to wake up each morning enthused about the coming day.

___I want a job I love or I want to love my job.

___I want a great relationship with my spouse and/or children.

___I want a more complete and fulfilling relationship with the Divine.

___I want (fill in the blank with something you want)
_____

There is no magic number of checked items that will give you the answer. You will have to look at what you checked and decide. I suggest that you ask yourself the question, If I changed the item(s) that I checked, how would my life change? Based on that answer, you will know if you want to put in the effort.

I would like to close the book by sharing with you a piece I wrote several years ago called "The Truth." It may help you find the answer to your questions.

The Truth

There once was born a magical child who had all the power the Divine could bestow on anyone. In order to keep his power, all he had to do was find the truth.

His mother said, "Listen to me and do it this way because I am your mother and I love you. I know the truth."

However, it never quite felt like it fit. And his power began to diminish.

His father said, "Listen to me; I know the truth because I have had a tough life, and look how successful I am. I have to go, but when I get home I will have time to finish this important talk with you."

However, it never quite felt like it fit. And his power continued to diminish.

His teachers said, "This is the way you must do things to get good grades. Listen to us because we know the truth, especially because we have read all of these books, and we are the experts."

However, it never quite felt like it fit. And his power continued to diminish.

At work, all of his bosses told him they knew the truth, and if he would listen to them he would go far. He would have more money and power than he could possibly handle.

However, it never quite felt like it fit. And his power continued to diminish.

He attended church after church and in each one the clergy told him, "Listen to me, for I know what God has in mind for you, and I am sure it is the truth."

However, it never quite felt like it fit. And his power continued to diminish.

As his life continued, he began to get very weary of the search for the truth. Time and again he asked his ego for help in finding the truth, and his ego always responded, "If only you acquired such and such, you will know the truth."

However, it never quite felt like it fit. And his power continued to diminish.

One day in a conversation with a wise coach, the coach asked him, "What is in your heart? For that is where you will find your truth."

When he asked his heart for the truth, his heart whispered in his ear and it fit. All of his power was unleashed!

It is only with the heart that one can see rightly; what is essential is invisible to the eye.—*The Little Prince*, Antoine de Saint-Exupery

Bibliography

Chapter 2

Frankl, Viktor. Man's Search for Meaning. Boston, MA: Beacon Press, 1984.

Childre, Doc and Howard Martin. The HeartMath Solution. San Francisco, CA: Harper San Francisco, 1999.

Neibuhr, Reinhold. http://en.wikipedia.org/wiki/Reinhold_Niebuhr#Serenity_Prayer.

Chapter 3

Williamson, Marianne. A Return to Love: Reflections on the Principles of "A Course in Miracles." New York, NY: HarperCollins, 1992.

Chapter 4

Lipton, Bruce. The Biology of Belief. Santa Rosa, CA: Mountain of Love/Elite Books, 2005.

Hill, Napoleon. Think and Grow Rich. Greenwich, CT: Fawcett Publications, 1963.

Childre, Doc, and Howard Martin. The HeartMath Solution. San Francisco, CA: Harper San Francisco, 1999.

Howard, Vernon. There is a Way Out. Pine, AZ: New Life Foundation, 2000.

Chapter 5

Pearsall, Paul, PhD. The Beethoven Factor. Charlottesville, VA: Hampton Roads Publishing, 2003.

Wattles, Wallace, D. The Science of Getting Rich. Scottsdale, AZ: LifeSuccess Productions, 1996.

Ruiz, Don Miguel. The Four Agreements. San Rafael, CA: Amber-Allen Publishing, Inc., 1997.

Gottman, John, PhD. The Heart of Parenting: Raising an Emotionally Intelligent Child. New York, NY, Fireside, 1997.

Seligman, Martin E.P. Authentic Happiness. New York, NY: Free Press, 2002.

Chapter 6

Karnazes, Dean. Ultramarathon Man: Confessions of an All-Night Runner. New York, NY: Jeremy P. Tarcher/Penguin, 2006.

Chapter 7

ThinkExist.com Quotations. "Earl Nightingale quotes." ThinkExist.com Quotations Online 1 May. 2011. 3 Jun. 2011 <http://einstein/quotes/earl_nightingale/2.html>

Chapter 8

Pearsall, Paul, PhD. The Beethoven Factor. Charlottesville, VA: Hampton Roads, 2003.

Buckingham, Marcus, and Donald O. Clifton. Now Discover Your Strengths. New York, NY: The Free Press, 2001.

Chapter 9

ThinkExist.com Quotations. "Tenzin Gyatso, The 14th Dalai Lama quotes." ThinkExist.com Quotations Online 1 May. 2011. 2 Jun. 2011. http://thinkexist.com/quotes/tenzin_gyatso,_the_14th_dalai_lama/.

Childre, Doc, and Howard Martin. The HeartMath Solution, New York, NY: Harper Collins Publishers Inc., 1999.

Chapter 10

Ashby, F. G., A. M. Isen, and U. Turken,. 1999. "A neuro-psychological theory of positive affect and its influence on cognition." Psychological Review, 106, 529–550.

Isen, A. M., T. Shalker, M. Clark, and L. Karp. 1978. "Affect, accessibility of material in memory and behavior: A cognitive loop?" Journal of Personality and Social Psychology, 36, 1–12.

Carnevale, P. J. D., and A. M. Isen. 1986. "The influence of positive affect and visual access on the discovery of integrative solutions in bilateral negotiation." Organizational Behavior and Human Decision Processes, 37, 1–13

Isen, A. M., and N. Geva. 1987. "The influence of positive affect on acceptable level of risk: The person with a large canoe has a large worry." Organizational Behavior and Human Decision Processes, 39, 145–154.

Wright, Thomas A., and Barry M. Staw. 1994. "In Search of the Happy/ Production Worker: A Longitudinal Study of Affect and Performance." Paper presented at the annual meeting of the Academy of Management, Dallas, Texas.

Estrada, C. A., A. M. Isen, and M. J. Young. 1997." Positive affect facilitates integration of information and decreases anchoring in reasoning among physicians." Organizational Behavior and Human Decision Processes 72, 117–135.

Danner, D. D., D. A. Snowdon, and W. V. Friesen. 2001. "Positive emotions in early life and longevity: Findings from the nun study." Journal of Personality and Social Psychology 80, 804–813.

Russek, L. G., and G. E. Schwartz. 1997. "Perceptions of parental caring predict health status in midlife: A 35-year follow-up of the Harvard Mastery of Stress Study." Psychosomatic Medicine 59, 144–149.

Goldman, Susan, A., Deborah T. Kraemer, and Peter Salovey. 1996. "Beliefs About Mood Moderate the Relationship of Stress to Illness and Symptom Reporting." Journal of Psychosomatic Research 41, (2): 115, 128.

Chapter 11

Jones, Laurie Beth. The Path. New York, NY: Hyperion Company, Inc., 1996.

Albom, Mitch. Tuesdays with Morrie. New York, NY: Doubleday, 1997

Chapter 12

Saint-Exupery, Antoine. The Little Prince. Orlando, FL: Harcourt Brace Jovanovich, Inc.,1943.

McCraty, Rollin, PhD and Doc Childre. The Appreciative Heart. Boulder Creek, CA: The Institute of HeartMath. http://dir.groups.yahoo.com/ group/veryquotablequotes/message/663

Gail Sheehy quote: www.brainyquote.com/quotes/quotes/g/ gailsheehy161346.html